Nouman Ali Khan

REVIVE YOUR HEART

Putting Life in Perspective

KUBE PUBLISHING

In association with

BAYYINAH

Revive Your Heart: Putting Life in Perspective

First published in England by
KUBE PUBLISHING LTD
Markfield Conference Centre
Ratby Lane, Markfield
Leicestershire LE67 9SY
United Kingdom
tel: +44 (0)1530 249230
fax: +44 (0)1530 249656
website: www.kubepublishing.com
email: info@kubepublishing.com

11th impression, 2025

CIP data for this book is available from the British Library.

ISBN 978-1-84774-107-3 *casebound*
ISBN 978-1-84774-101-1 *paperback*
ISBN 978-1-84774-104-2 *ebook*

Arabic & English typeset by: N A Qaddoura
Cover artwork: Iman Anwar
Cover design by: Fatima Jamadar
Printed by: Elma Basim, Turkey

Contents

Transliteration Table v

Preface vi

Part I

Connecting to Allah Through *Du'ā'*

1. A Prayer for Desperate Times 3
2. *Du'ā'* and Disappointment 22

Part II

Creating a Cohesive Muslim Community

3. Criticism 45
4. Assumptions 65
5. Leadership 82

Part III

Our Financial Dealings

6. How We Earn 107
7. Money Matters 127

Part IV
Some Contemporary Issues

8. It's a Girl! 149
9. Thoughts on Paris 170
10. *Naṣīḥah* in Brief: The Dangers of Listening to Music 192

Part V
Focusing on the *Ākhirah*

11. Putting Life in Perspective 199
12. Small Beginnings 216
13. *Naṣīḥah* in Brief: The Afterlife 240

Glossary 246

Transliteration Table

Arabic Consonants

Initial, unexpressed medial and final: ء ʼ

ا a	د d	ض ḍ	ك k
ب b	ذ dh	ط ṭ	ل l
ت t	ر r	ظ ẓ	م m
ث th	ز z	ع ʻ	ن n
ج j	س s	غ gh	هـ h
ح ḥ	ش sh	ف f	و w
خ kh	ص ṣ	ق q	ي y

Vowels, diphthongs, etc.

Short:	a ـَ	i ـِ	u ـُ
Long:	ā ـَا	ī ـِي	ū ـُو
Diphthongs:	aw ـَوْ		
	ay ـَيْ		

Preface

The world today is abuzz with unrelenting activity. The developments in the worlds of politics, economics, social media, entertainment, technology and beyond, are all constantly vying for our attention. But more importantly, they are vying to distract our hearts. In line with the ideology of unfettered free markets, we are constantly being 'exhorted' to consume. There has, perhaps, never been a time when Allah's words, *alhākum al-takāthur* (*al-Takāthur* 102: 1), were more applicable. We have arrived at a time when being distracted from our duties to Allah has been institutionalized: the entertainment industry is undoubtedly one of the most imposing industries of modernity.

Of course, it does not stop there. In modern society, individuals can be reduced to little more than atomized consumers. Our *dīn* also can become commodified into a form of entertainment in this environment. Our scholars can become celebrities, who we watch for a 'spiritual high' before returning to our routinized consumer existence. The

Muslim ummah is experiencing crises of religious identity, with its global image being hijacked by violent groups. These groups attract young Muslims, ignorant of their *dīn*, into their ranks through their domination of the headlines with shocking acts of violence.

With such levels of distraction and crisis, it is difficult to stay spiritually centred. Our communities and mosques are not always the centres of spiritual guidance and counsel we need them to be. The Prophet taught us: *al-dīn al-naṣīḥah*—"The *dīn* is about giving sincere counsel." And in an age of distraction and pervasive negativity, positive and constructive reminders are essential to our spiritual well-being.

This collection of reminders from *Ustādh* Nouman Ali Khan is an important contribution in our age of distraction. *Ustādh* Nouman's reminders speak directly to the heart, encouraging us to be mindful of our duties to Allah, exhorting us to put life in perspective. Contemporary culture asks us to think of death as the ultimate conclusion to what should be a hedonistic existence, while our *dīn* teaches us that death is only the beginning of our true lives.

The subtitle of this work, *Putting Life in Perspective*, is about reminding ourselves not to forget the true nature of reality. Our lives here are temporary. They are the small window of opportunity to do some good in the world for which Allah will judge whether we are deserving of *jannah*. The author deals with issues from the highly personal to the global. The work is divided into five parts with two or three reminders in each. They range from the profoundly personal questions of how we should approach Allah in our prayers, and how we should never think ill of our fellows; to communal ills such as the unacceptable attitude many Muslim communities have towards daughters, despite the explicit teachings of the Prophet that honour daughters, and women generally.

Ustādh Nouman's work is also an excellent example of what Muslim communities and their scholars need to do in reaching out to a global audience through the building of institutions like Bayyinah, and the harnessing of modern social media to reach people from all walks of life. It is immensely important that modern Muslims and, in particular, Muslims in the West, invest in institutions that will promote sound Islamic teachings to counteract the rise in extremism that has engulfed parts of the world where traditional institutions of learning have been reduced to ruin by imperial wars and corrupt scholars.

It is hoped that this work will contribute to inspiring modern Muslims to become sources of light in our world through the revival of their hearts, and the reorientation of their outlooks towards greater social responsibility and greater God-consciousness.

The Editor, Kube Publishing Ltd.
January 2017

PART I

CONNECTING TO ALLAH THROUGH DU‘Ā’

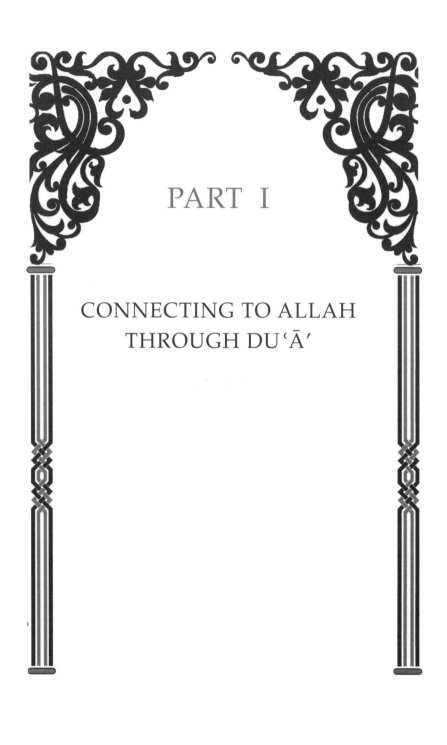

CHAPTER 1

A Prayer for Desperate Times

In this reminder, *in shā' Allāh ta'ālā*, I would like to share with you some reflections on an *āyah* from *Sūrat al-Qaṣaṣ*, the twenty-eighth surah of the Qur'an. The story of *Mūsā* (*'alayhi al-salām*) is mentioned in many places in the Qur'an. In this particular place, Allah is telling us about the part of his life before he speaks with Allah on the mountain of Ṭūr. Glimpses of the life of *Mūsā* (*'alayhi al-salām*) before that event are captured in *Sūrat al-Qaṣaṣ*. One of those events is when he escaped Egypt and made it into Madyan. He escaped because he was wanted for murder; even though it was a mistake. He had punched someone, and they had died by accident. He had escaped the city, escaped Egypt because they were looking for him and were going to kill him if they found him. The order was 'shoot to kill'.

Allah guided him through the desert and He got him all the way to the waters of Madyan. Madyan is in the middle of the desert but it has some waters, some lakes and ponds, so he ends up over there; finally sitting, getting some relief, drinking some water. Allah (*ʿazza wa-jall*) tells us that:

... وَجَدَ عَلَيْهِ أُمَّةً مِّنَ ٱلنَّاسِ يَسْقُونَ وَوَجَدَ مِن دُونِهِمُ ٱمْرَأَتَيْنِ تَذُودَانِ ... ﴿٢٣﴾

(القصص ٢٨ : ٢٣)

> ... he found there a crowd of people watering their flocks, and he found apart from them two women holding their flocks back ...
>
> (Al-Qaṣaṣ 28: 23)

He found a group of people that were giving their animals drink and besides them he saw two women who were pulling on their animals. In other words, up on top of the hill there are two young ladies that had some animals but they are not letting their animals drink the water, while all the rest of the village is feeding their animals water: their sheep and their goats and their camels and their cows are all drinking water. But these women with their sheep, they are just tugging away at them. Obviously the sheep see the water so they want to go drink; but they're not going, they are staying in place.

He sees this scene so he goes up to them and says:

... قَالَ مَا خَطْبُكُمَا قَالَتَا لَا نَسْقِي حَتَّىٰ يُصْدِرَ ٱلرِّعَآءُ وَأَبُونَا شَيْخٌ كَبِيرٌ ﴿٢٣﴾

(القصص ٢٨ : ٢٣)

> ... He asked the women: "What is it that troubles you?" They said: "We cannot water our flocks until the shepherds take their flocks away, and our father is a very old man."
>
> (Al-Qaṣaṣ 28: 23)

'What's wrong with you two? What's the situation here?' And they said, 'We don't give our flock drink from this pond until the entire flock of the people is done'. What they are trying to say is we don't want to go among those men because a lot of them are perverts; they don't respect women. They howl at us or they harass us so we would rather all of these people finish, because they are a bunch of idiots, and then we will do our work. Our father is an old man: and one of the meanings of the *āyah—wa-abūnā shaykh kabīr*—is a very old man; meaning he cannot do this work anymore, we are the only ones in the family that can do this work.

So *Mūsā* (*ʿalayhi al-salām*) doesn't continue talking to them, he actually just grabs the sheep, goes to the well, and moves those guys like they were a bunch of insects because he is a very strong man. He fed the animals and brought them back. This is the *āyah* that I want to reflect on with you in this reminder, this brief background was there so everybody's on the same page.

فَسَقَىٰ لَهُمَا ثُمَّ تَوَلَّىٰٓ إِلَى ٱلظِّلِّ فَقَالَ رَبِّ إِنِّي لِمَآ أَنزَلْتَ إِلَيَّ مِنْ خَيْرٍ فَقِيرٌ ﴿٢٤﴾

(القصص ٢٨ : ٢٤)

… Moses watered their flocks for them, and then returned in a shaded place and said: "My Lord, I am truly in great need of any good that You might send down to me."

(Al-Qaṣaṣ 28: 24)

He watered and fed their animals for them. Thereafter, he turned back to the shade. So now *Mūsā* (*ʿalayhi al-salām*) goes back and lies down or relaxes under the shade again, once he sits down what does he do? One of the most famous *duʿā*s in the entire Qur'an: he turns to Allah and says, 'My Master, no doubt about it, whatever good you have sent down my way, whatever you have descended—sent down towards me—of any kind of good; no doubt about it, I am desperately in need of it'. This is the *duʿā'* of *Mūsā* (*ʿalayhi al-salām*) when he sat back down in the shade.

I wanted to take the opportunity in this reminder to discuss with you some of the benefits of this incredible statement; so powerful that Allah (*ʿazza wa-jall*) made it a part of His Qur'an. As long as Muslims are around we are going to be celebrating this *duʿā'* of *Mūsā* (*ʿalayhi al-salām*) that he made in private, there were no congregations behind him, he wasn't saying this *duʿā'* and there were thousands of people behind him saying *āmīn;* he's just by himself, sitting under the shade of a tree, making this *du'ā'* but this *du'ā'* is so valuable to Allah that until *yawm al-qiyāmah* we're going to be reciting this *du'ā'* and we are going to be celebrating these remarkable words.

The first thing I would like to share with you here is that when you help people, you don't wait around until they say thank you because you didn't help them so you can hear appreciation. When *Mūsā* (*'alayhi al-salām*) helped those ladies, you don't find in the Qur'an: 'They both said thank you so much', and he said: 'No problem, no big deal'. He didn't expect and he didn't actually continue the conversation with them, he handed over the animals and walked away. He did this for Allah and so the only one he wants to get appreciation from is Allah. He's not interested in a conversation with those two women; he is interested in a conversation with Allah. A lot of times we do good things but in the back of our head we're hoping to get some recognition, we're hoping to get some appreciation, some other side benefits; we are going to learn in this *du'ā'* that if you make your intentions pure, you help someone, you do something good for someone but you expect and converse only with Allah, then Allah will take more care of you than you could ever imagine.

Obviously, sometimes people do each other favours because they are hoping if I do you a favour today, maybe tomorrow you will do me a favour. I'm doing this for you hoping you're going to do something for me—I scratch your back, you scratch mine. But in this *du'ā'*, you notice, even though *Mūsā* (*'alayhi al-salām*) is homeless, he's a fugitive from the law, he has no clothes other than the ones he is wearing on his back, he has no provisions with him—clearly he is stopping at this pond to drink some water because he doesn't even have food and drink. He's pretty much at the point of desperation, as desperate as a human being can get. And yet, when he helps these women, he doesn't expect from them; he still expects from Allah. When you do something voluntarily, because he volunteered, right? He didn't say, 'Well how much are you going to pay me?'

By the way that was work, and if you do work, it's okay for you to ask for wages—it's not a problem. If you do work for someone it doesn't have to be voluntary. But he volunteered himself, which means once you offer yourself voluntarily, don't expect compensation. If you are expecting compensation, bring that up from the very beginning. Say from the very beginning, 'Look, I need to get paid for this'. A lot of times, for example, we volunteer for projects or for the masjid and in the back of our heads we're thinking, 'I volunteered the entire month of Ramadan. On the twenty-seventh they are going to have an award ceremony for me; they are going to hand me something; they are going to give me some appreciation.' Even if that expectation is in our head, we are missing something from this *duʿā'*. We cannot have that expectation. *Mūsā* (*ʿalayhi al-salām*) turns away from them and sits back down under the shade, he talks to Allah and he says to Allah some of the most incredible words in the Qur'an:

.... رَبِّ إِنِّي لِمَآ أَنزَلْتَ إِلَيَّ مِنْ خَيْرٍ فَقِيرٌ ﴿٢٤﴾
(القصص ٢٨ : ٢٤)

... "My Lord, I am truly in great need of any good that You might send down to me."

(Al-Qaṣaṣ 28: 24)

Rabbī innī limā anzalta ilayya min khayrin faqīr: Master, whatever you sent down my way—and this is in the past tense, I did not say whatever you 'send' down my way but whatever you 'sent' down my way: *anzalta*. Whatever you already sent down, I was in desperate need of it. In other words this shade and that water in front of him, that's all he gets right now. He doesn't have a house, he doesn't have food, he doesn't have anything else; and yet he is looking at all of this and telling Allah, '*Yā Allāh*, thank you so much for this; I desperately needed it'. In other words, before asking Allah for more, he is concentrating on what Allah has already given him.

If you look at it from our perspective, he has nothing. He's got absolutely nothing! But from his perspective, he was in the middle of the desert and there is no logical reason why he couldn't have died of dehydration. The fact that he made it all the way to the water, and the fact that he found a place to sit which is under a shade, which Allah mentions—*thumma tawallā ilā al-ẓill*; the fact that he found that much and on top of all of this the fact that he found an opportunity to do a good deed is enough for him to be grateful. Instead of thinking about what he doesn't have, he turns to Allah and says, basically, I'll put it in easy language for you: '*Yā Allāh*, I really needed that, thanks! I really needed that; I was so desperate, I would have died without this help of yours'—*Rabbī innī limā anzalta ilayya min khayrin faqīr*.

Subḥān Allāh! What a different attitude—he is constantly thinking about what he has to be grateful for.

Now there is more meaning to this *duʿā'*; the other piece of this *duʿā'* that's remarkable is that *Mūsā* (*ʿalayhi al-salām*), not too long ago, accidentally killed somebody. He punched someone while he was defending another man, and the Coptic soldier of *Firʿawn* (Pharaoh) die. And so he's run from this and, by the way, he felt guilty about what happened. He made *duʿā'* to Allah to forgive him for what happened, but he still feels guilt inside of him. When you feel guilty inside of you, what should you do? This is a lesson about making mistakes, all of us have made mistakes in our lives; all of us pretty much have done things that aren't exactly what Allah expected us to do. What do you do after you make a mistake? And by the way, some of our mistakes are small and some of our mistakes are very big. The mistake that *Mūsā* (*ʿalayhi al-salām*) made is to take another person's life; that is not a small mistake. If you or I made that kind of a mistake, we would have a hard time sleeping for the rest of our lives. If you have any conscience, this would be the kind of thing that could haunt you for the rest of your life; you would not be able to get over it. It's not something you would just forget about.

Say you spoke ill of someone, or you lost your temper, or maybe you forgot at the time and you did some backbiting or whatever, these are mistakes; but you forget about them. You don't remember what you did two years ago, you forget. But if you accidentally killed someone, that's serious business. So what I am trying to tell you is that we, you and I, have made mistakes in our past; but for some of us those mistakes are so big in our mind, we are never able to move on with life. We are never able to think past that mistake—we're constantly thinking about that mistake. This *duʿā'* is teaching us that if you have a mistake in your past, if you've done something really bad in your past—and I'm pretty confident that it's not the same as the mistake of *Mūsā* (*'alayhi al-salām*); I'm pretty sure that the police aren't out looking for you for murder—anything short of that you should be covered. Allah gave us this extreme example, so that we could understand, if Allah will cover that one; then I'm covered, I'm okay, mine is not as bad. So now, what is the lesson here? The lesson here is that if you have made a mistake then you should be desperate to find opportunities to do good things for people.

Mūsā (*'alayhi al-salām*) is almost dead from dehydration and starvation, he's barely surviving, and he sees two women in need of help. What does he do? He gets up and helps them. Why in the world would he get up and—they didn't ask for help; he just sees this opportunity. He didn't say: 'Okay, let me just get a little bit of a rest and then maybe I will figure out what is going on over there'; or he could have just assumed on his own: they are waiting for these men to finish. He's a smart man, he could figure all of this out himself. But the fact that he felt the urge to go and help them is because he is desperate to help. If you have any mistakes in your past there should be a fire inside of you to want to do good things. Every time there is an opportunity, no matter how tired you are, no matter how exhausted you are, no matter how unmotivated you are, you motivate yourself. And what should motivate you? The mistake of your past.

So one of the meanings of this *du'ā'* is: '*Yā Allāh*, I've made a pretty bad mistake in my past so whatever opportunity you give me to make up for it, I will take it. I could desperately use that. So thank you so much for giving me the chance, the honour of helping these women'. Please listen to that again, 'Thank you for giving me the honour of helping these women'. When you help someone, you are not honouring them; they are honouring you. In our *dīn* when you give *ṣadaqah*, for example to someone begging outside, you give charity; you have not helped them, the fact of the matter is they have helped you. They become testimony for you on Judgement Day. They become a forgiveness of your sins. You've helped them only in the *dunyā*, which is nothing to Allah, but they have helped you in *ākhirah*, which is everything. This is the change of attitude. This is: *Rabbī innī limā anzalta ilayya min khayrin faqīr*.

But also in this *du'ā'*, the final and equally important piece is that when he makes this *du'ā'*, *Mūsā* (*'alayhi al-salām*) is acknowledging that whatever he has, he has to be grateful for. But at the same time, *Mūsā* (*'alayhi al-salām*) knows better than any of us—because we're not in the middle of the desert dying—that he is in need of food, he is in need of shelter, he is in need of protection, he is in need of a job, he is in need of these things, but the interesting thing is he doesn't ask Allah for any of them. We should ask Allah for everything. Why doesn't he ask Allah?, '*Yā Allāh* feed me, *yā Allāh* give me more, *yā Allāh* provide me a house, yā *Allāh* fix my life up; I've got a problem'. Why doesn't he ask for any of it? You see, in saying to Allah that whatever you have given me, I desperately needed it; he has actually asked Allah. Please try to understand the subtlety of this statement.

I'll give you this example to help you understand this concept, because it's a very profound concept in our religion. Our children sometimes they are picky and fussy about what they want to eat, you put vegetables on the dinner table and say to your son sitting there: 'eat your carrots'. He responds: 'No, I don't want to eat carrots, I want chocolate'. So he doesn't want the carrots, he wants chocolate; he doesn't want to drink the water, he wants juice; he doesn't want to finish the food, he wants ice-cream first. In other words what you give him, he doesn't want and what he doesn't have, he wants. And do you get upset or not? You get a bit: 'Why don't you appreciate what I have done? You need this food. You're going to get sick, you need this medicine. You need this dinner. Finish your food, that's not good for you', but he wants what's not good for him and he doesn't care for what is in front of him.

The believer recognizes that whatever Allah gives you, whatever food He put on the table, whatever job you found, whatever business your doing—not only is it good enough; you desperately needed it. You don't get to be fussy with Allah and tell him, '*Yā Allāh*, I don't know if I want this one'. You don't get to tell Allah, 'I know You provided me this rock or this tree to sit under but if You could provide me some kind of bedding, it would be better'. 'I know You gave me this water over here but maybe some coconuts might help'. No, no, no. Whatever You have given me, is exactly what I needed and I desperately needed it. I desperately needed it. What word does he use to describe himself? He uses the word *'faqīr'*—*innī limā anzalta ilayya min khayrin faqīr*. Do you know the difference between *faqīr* and *miskīn*? Another word in the Qur'an for someone who is bankrupt, someone who can't help themselves is *miskīn*. Allah says:

﴿ إِنَّمَا ٱلصَّدَقَـٰتُ لِلْفُقَرَآءِ وَٱلْمَسَـٰكِينِ ... ﴾ (التوبة ٩ : ٦٠)

The alms are meant only for the poor and the needy...

(Al-Tawbah 9: 60)

Allah put those two together, meaning you're supposed to give *ṣadaqah* to the one who is *faqīr* and to the one who is *miskīn*, and when you put two words together like that, it means, they mean two different things. According to Ibn Manẓūr in *Lisān al-ʿArab*, the *faqīr* is in the worst possible situation; the *miskīn* might even own some things. That's why in the Qur'an, in *Sūrat al-Kahf*, the *masākīn* own a ship:

أَمَّا ٱلسَّفِينَةُ فَكَانَتْ لِمَسَٰكِينَ يَعْمَلُونَ فِى ٱلْبَحْرِ ... ﴿٧٩﴾
(الكهف ١٨ : ٧٩)

As for the boat it belonged to some poor people who worked on the river...

(Al-Kahf 18: 79)

Even if someone is *miskīn*, they might still own a boat, they might still be fishermen, they might still have a job; but a *faqīr*: He's got nothing! He's got absolutely nothing. He says to Allah that I have absolutely nothing.

They say in Arabic: 'the one who is walking is happy with whatever ride he can get'. You know what they mean by that? If there is a guy walking in the middle of the desert and somebody offers him a donkey, or somebody offers him a horse, or somebody offers him a turtle to sit on, he won't mind. He's not going to say, 'I don't know if this is my kind of ride. I need a more luxury class vehicle'. He's not going to say that. He'll say: 'Give me that bicycle, I'll take it!' Because he has nothing. He is turning to Allah and saying, '*Yā Allāh*, I acknowledge that I have absolutely nothing. And I don't even have a means to earn anything. You are the only one who sent this down my way; I am not going to complain'.

The point I am trying to make is just coming. When he made this *du'ā'* to Allah, when he turned to Allah and said, *'Yā Allāh* my back is broken'. A *faqīr*, by the way, is also someone whose back is broken. When your back is broken it means you cannot lift anything; things have to be given to you because you cannot even go and get them. That's why he said, *'Yā Allāh,* whatever you sent towards me is because I'm *faqīr*, I can't go and get it. You are bringing it to me!' *Subḥān Allāh*, this is the acknowledgment of *Mūsā* (*'alayhi al-salām*).

When he makes this *du'ā'*, the next *āyah* of *Sūrat al-Qaṣaṣ* is:

فَجَآءَتْهُ إِحْدَىٰهُمَا تَمْشِى عَلَى ٱسْتِحْيَآءٍ قَالَتْ إِنَّ أَبِى يَدْعُوكَ لِيَجْزِيَكَ أَجْرَ مَا سَقَيْتَ لَنَا ... ﴿٢٥﴾

(القصص ٢٨ : ٢٥)

> Soon thereafter one of the two women came to him, walking bashfully, and said: "My father invites you that he may reward you for your having watered our flocks for us..."
>
> (Al-Qaṣaṣ 28: 25)

'Therefore', listen carefully now, 'therefore one of those two girls came back and said, "my father wants to pay you".' The word 'therefore' is important. Did he ask for money? No. Did he ask for a job? No. Did he ask to be invited to their house? No. None of this, he only turned to Allah and said whatever you have given me, I was desperately in need of it, I appreciate it. You turn to Allah in appreciation and as a result, there's a formula, there's a rule. You know how we call them the laws of nature; there are laws of Qur'an and they are more powerful than the laws of nature. The laws of nature change: fire is supposed to burn but it will stop burning when *Ibrahim* (*ʿalayhi al-salām*) is thrown inside; water is supposed to retain its shape but it will change when *Mūsā* (*ʿalayhi al-salām*) strikes his staff and Allah makes the water not keep its shape. The laws of nature can bend when Allah wants them to but the laws of Allah in His book, the laws of guidance, they don't bend. The laws of *duʿā'*, they don't bend. And what is this law? That when you appreciate what Allah has given you, then Allah will take care of you!

What happens? She comes to him and says, 'My dad wants to pay you'. He doesn't turn to her and say, 'No thank you sister, I did that *fī sabīl Allah*, I don't want any money'. He understood immediately that this is Allah responding to his *duʿā'*. He did not have what we call back home, where I come from, *takalluf*: 'No, no, no, thank you. I don't need anything, I don't need it'. When people are offering you help, that might be from Allah, that might be the answer to your *duʿā'*. So if somebody is offering you a job and you say, 'No, no, no, I can't accept this favour', why are you turning away the favour of Allah? *Mūsā* (*ʿalayhi al-salām*) has far more integrity than you, he didn't shy away and say, 'No, no, no, that was a voluntary task, I expect nothing'. He expected nothing; he expected from whom? From Allah. But when Allah brings people his way, he doesn't turn it down.

As I conclude, let me tell you what happens. This one *duʿā'* that he made, with that sincerity: not only did he get invited, not only did he get paid, as a matter of fact in the middle of that conversation he got offered the daughter's hand in marriage; so he got married and on top of that he got a job for eight to ten years. So he got housing, employment, marriage, immigration status, all of it in one shot, because of this one *duʿā'*! Did he ask for any of these things? No. He started his entire family—a new life began for *Mūsā* (*ʿalayhi al-salām*) all because he appreciated what Allah (*ʿazza wa-jall*) had given him, even in the middle of the desert, even in the middle of nothing.

We have to become a people of *shukr*; a people of gratitude. Which is why you must appreciate that when *Mūsā* (*ʿalayhi al-salām*) is in a desert again. *Mūsā* (*ʿalayhi al-salām*) ends up in a desert twice: once when he ran away as an individual from the army and a second time when he ran away from the armies of *Firʿawn* as the leader of an entire nation. So in the life of *Mūsā* (*ʿalayhi al-salām*) he ends up escaping from Egypt twice: once, personally; once, with an entire nation. When he left with his entire nation, you know what he said to them? He said to them:

وَإِذْ تَأَذَّنَ رَبُّكُمْ لَئِن شَكَرْتُمْ لَأَزِيدَنَّكُمْ ... ﴿٧﴾

(إبراهيم ١٤ : ٧)

Also call to mind when your Lord proclaimed: "If you give thanks, I will certainly grant you more..."

(Ibrahim 14: 7)

He turns to the Israelites who are in the middle of the desert, complaining about the heat, complaining about the lack of food, complaining about the lack of water. He turns to them and says, 'Your Master had already declared that, "if you can become grateful, I will absolutely increase you".' I will give you more and more and more. *Mūsā* (*ʿalayhi al-salām*) is not just teaching them a theory; he is teaching them this *duʿā'* based on his life experience. He's already done this before. When he was grateful to Allah, Allah gave him more and more and more and more. This is the life lesson he is teaching the *Banī Isrā'īl*, and that *duʿā'*—*la'in shakartum la'azīdannakum*—is so powerful; it was a *khuṭbah* given by *Mūsā* (*ʿalayhi al-salām*) to *Banī Isrā'īl*, and even that got recorded in the Qur'an.

So you and I have to learn—and this is something we easily forget—to be grateful for what we do have, and not to focus our attention so much on what we don't have. To learn to acknowledge that whatever we do have, we could not have survived without it, we are *faqīr* for it. When we really, internally, develop that attitude, as a result of that Allah will provide us the whole *dunyā* and whatever is in it. Allah will give without restriction.

... إِنَّمَا يُوَفَّى ٱلصَّـٰبِرُونَ أَجْرَهُم بِغَيْرِ حِسَابٍ ﴿١٠﴾
(الزّمر ٣٩: ١٠)

... Verily those who persevere shall be granted their reward beyond all reckoning.

(Al-Zumar 39: 10)

The people of *ṣabr* are going to be paid without any restrictions. May Allah (*ʿazza wa-jall*) help us to internalize this beautiful, remarkable *duʿā'*.

CHAPTER 2

Du'ā' and Disappointment

This reminder is actually inspired by a number of conversations I've had the opportunity to have with young people and old people alike, on a subject that is central to the life of every Muslim—that subject matter is *du'ā'*. A lot of people come up to me and say, 'I'm trying to make so much *du'ā'* because there's this one thing I am trying to get'. When it's a young man; it's a girl he wants to marry, or a job he is looking for that he really wants to get, or immigration papers to be sorted out. If it's somebody a little bit older, sometimes it's *du'ā'* for their children to be guided. Their children have become rebellious; they're not praying any more, they're not listening to their parents anymore and the mother comes to me crying and says, 'I make lots of *du'ā'* for my son, I've been making it for years but nothing is changing. Things are not getting better, things are getting worse. What am I supposed to do? Why is my *du'ā'* not working?'

There are people that come to me and say, 'I've been sick and I'm getting sicker and sicker. I even made umrah and I went to hajj and I made *duʿāʾ* at the *Ḥaram*, and I went to *al-Masjid al-Nabawī*, and I am making *duʿāʾ* in the middle of the night, and I am praying all night, but my *duʿā*s are not getting answered. What am I supposed to do?' And then there are people who say: I used to make *duʿāʾ*, I used to pray to Allah. Like this very interesting young man I met. He said, 'Man, I didn't even pray a lot but I had this exam, it was really hard so I decided that I am going to make a lot of *duʿā*s so I even like prayed and stuff. I prayed for a whole ten minutes and I still failed; so I don't pray anymore, because I didn't get what I was looking for.'

So my own analysis after a lot of these conversations is that there is actually a real confusion about what *duʿāʾ* actually means. What does it mean that we are asking Allah for something? From what position are we asking? Is asking Allah the same as asking your parents or asking somebody else? If it's not the same, how is it different? What are we supposed to expect when we make *duʿāʾ* to Allah (*ʿazza wa-jall*)?

There seems to be, among the average Muslim, a lot of confusion about this very simple and very fundamental thing. As a matter of fact the centre of our religion is *duʿāʾ*. The Fatihah which is the opening of the Qur'an and is the heart of the Qur'an is itself a *duʿāʾ*. Every prophet (*ʿalayhim al-salām*) that Allah talks about in the Qur'an makes *du'ā'*. Every one of them; it's their lasting legacy. We may not know every detail: *Nūḥ* (*'alayhi al-salām*) lived 950 years among his people. We don't know all the details of those 950 years, but we do know the *du'ās*, Allah recorded those. We don't know a lot about *Yūnus* (*'alayhi al-salām*), but we do know his *du'ās*. We don't know a lot, we know a few more things about *Ibrahim* (*'alayhi al-salām*), but we definitely know his *du'ās*. If there is one thing Allah definitely tells us about the prophets (*'alayhim al-salām*) it is the prayers they made, the way they asked Allah. So it's a pretty big deal in our religion.

One of the greatest prophetic traditions is the tradition of *du'ā'*. There is virtually a prayer for every act that you and I do, from going into our home, to changing our clothes, to greeting each other, to getting married. I mean there is not an occasion in life that doesn't come with a prophetic prayer, it's incredible. So it is at the centre of our religion and to have confusion about this is a pretty big deal.

I wanted to address this, even though this is a topic that is much bigger than such a brief reminder. But I wanted to give you some basic pointers from a couple of *āyāt* of the Qur'an. The first two of them belong to *Sūrat Maryam*. In *Sūrat Maryam* we see the prayers of different prophets but there are two of them that I'm going to highlight to you.

قَالَ رَبِّ إِنِّي وَهَنَ ٱلْعَظْمُ مِنِّي وَٱشْتَعَلَ ٱلرَّأْسُ شَيْبًا وَلَمْ أَكُنْ بِدُعَآئِكَ رَبِّ شَقِيًّا ﴿٤﴾

(مريم ١٩ : ٤)

He said: "Lord! My bones have grown feeble and my head is glistening with age; yet, never have my prayers to You, my Lord, been unfruitful".

(Maryam 19: 4)

In the beginning of the surah is *Zakariyyā* (*ʿalayhi al-salām*) who's reaching old age—*innī wahana al-ʿaẓm minnī*—he says literally: 'My bones are getting weak and they are rebelling against me'. This '*min*' is *min al-tabʿīḍ*. You know in modern medicine when the bones and the joints aren't as strong as they used to be, and people feel the arthritis or whatever in their joints, this is literally what he is talking about. It takes him a while to make *rukūʿ*; it's not easy for him to sit down. Young men, they get up and down without a problem; but when your bones become weak, and if you see an old man or an old woman take a seat, it takes them a while to sit down. They can't just sit down. It takes them a while to get out of bed they can't just spring out of bed like young guys. Some young people fall out of bed and then get up, no problem. But when an older person whose bones have become weak falls; they end up in the ER. It's very serious for them. So he senses the weakness in his bones, that's where this conversation with Allah begins: *innī wahana al-ʿaẓm minnī wa-shtaʿala al-ra's shayban*—and my hair is like a fire went on my head and all that's left is ash. Ash is grey and white, so he looks at his head and says, 'My head used to be black and now it's just white, that's all that's left'. There is a saying in Arabic: *shaybuka nāʿīk*—that you're greying hair or your whitening hair is the alarm of your death. In other words every time you look at your grey hair, it's one more hair towards, one more step towards death.

So he begins the *duʿā'* by talking about his frailty—he's gotten very old. He realizes he's close to death and then he says something. I won't even tell you about his *duʿā*s, it's his attitude towards *duʿā'*. He says: *wa-lam akun bi-duʿāika Rabbi shaqiyyā*—I have never, ever been miserable, I have never been in a bad mood, I've never been unhappy calling you. Whenever I ask you, I've always been happy. I've never had depression when I've made *duʿā'* to you. That's what he is saying looking back at his entire life. By the way, this is the man who doesn't have a child. He's old, he's got grey hair now, he's about to die, his bones are weak, and one of the sad things in an old man's life is that he has no one to carry his name. So you can imagine this is not the first time he's making *duʿā'* for a child. He's been making *duʿā'* his whole life but he says I was never depressed when I asked you. I have never been *shaqī* when I asked you. When you check the lexicons of the Arabic language for the word *shaqī*, or *shiqāwah* and *shaqāwah*—both are found in the Arabic language—and *shiqwah* also, they say it's *ḍidd al-saʿāda*—the opposite of happiness. It has the meanings of grief, sadness, it has the meanings of depression. It's also used for a sadness or a bad mood that is short or long term—*yumadd wa-yuqṣar*, they say in Arabic. It could be something that is extended like some of you know people in your family that are just always in a bad mood—that's long term *shaqī*. Then there are some people that just get in a bad mood sometimes, either way this term applies.

This statement that he made is actually incredibly powerful in teaching us something about our attitude when we make *duʿāʾ* to Allah. Who are we asking anyway? We're asking our *Rabb*, and usually we ask when we feel the need for something we don't have. That's probably true for most people, right? You're at the verge of something like—*maʿādh Allāh*—one of our children is going to see the doctor; we make *duʿāʾ* for the health of our child. You're going into a job interview, you turn and you make *duʿāʾ* to Allah—'*Yā Allāh*, this interview; I really need this job'. You're about to sign papers for a house, '*Yā Allāh*, put *barakah* in this house. *Yā Allāh*, this is a pretty big deal, this is a serious investment I'm getting into'. So when you make *duʿāʾ*; you make *duʿāʾ* because you get to a point in life where you seriously need something and you realize it.

But let's take a step back, every single day you and I wake up and we did not have to have a respirator on for our lungs to keep working all night. Every single night when we went to sleep, our heart was still beating. Every single day when we got out of bed, we opened our eyes and we could still see; our ears could still hear, and *wa-Llāhi*, they're not on autopilot. They're not running on energizer batteries. This is Allah providing you and me with another breath, another heartbeat, another day to move our limbs. Yet the only time we turn to Allah is when we need something; when we feel we're missing something. But as a matter of fact, Allah is constantly providing you and me without us even asking. We don't have to make *duʿā'* to Allah to be able to breathe, can you imagine how that would be? We don't have to make *duʿā'* to Allah to be able to hear; to be able to see; to be able to speak. Imagine every time I have to speak, make *duʿā'* to Allah then He gives my tongue the ability, then I can say something.

Subḥān Allāh, there are a lot of things Allah gives us that we absolutely need—we *absolutely* need—we cannot survive without them and yet He provides, and He provides, and He provides. So what I am trying to get at first is, before you and I think about what Allah did not give me—How come He didn't give me this? How come He didn't answer this *duʿā'* or that *duʿā'* and that *duʿā'*? Allah says: *kulla yawmin huwa fī sha'n* (*al-Raḥmān* 55: 29)—everyday He is involved in giving you something. He is engaged in providing me, and providing me, and providing me, and providing you.

So when someone becomes wretched or miserable or in a bad mood about *duʿāʾ* maybe they haven't understood what Allah has been doing for them all along.

I'll make it easy for you to understand. Your mother loves you. Those of you that are fortunate enough that your mother is alive, and you are fortunate enough that she lives in your country or you get to visit her. When you go visit your mother after a long time—and she is getting old now—she makes you food, she puts it on the table and she gives you a hug. You start eating the food and you say, 'Mum where's the salt? Come on! Don't you know!? I need some extra salt. Where's the ketchup? You didn't even get the ketchup!? And I thought you were going to get me Pepsi, you only bought 7-Up?' What kind of miserable person are you that your mother does all of this for you and you can only think about what's missing? You can think about what she didn't do. That shows you have no appreciation for what your mother does for you, and what she has been doing for you, and the love and care she put into providing for you.

That's just you and your mother. We're talking about Allah (*ʿazza wa-jall*). We're talking about someone whose love cannot be measured, and it can't be quantified. People ask the question, 'How come Allah doesn't listen to my *duʿāʾ*?' That is a very offensive question. To Allah it is a very offensive question. How in the world do you say that He doesn't listen?

Allah (*ʿazza wa-jall*), He doesn't just say He listens, He responds to every *duʿāʾ*. But then how come He didn't respond in the way I wanted and the way you wanted. That's the real question I'm going to try to answer.

I want to make sure we understand in this reminder what *duʿāʾ* is not? *Duʿāʾ* is not placing an order at a restaurant. *Duʿāʾ* is not placing an order for a product. When you place an order, you pay something and you get what you expected. You place an order for French fries; you're not supposed to get a burger. You're supposed to get French fries. When you place an order for a laptop, you're not supposed to get a phone in the mail. You get what you ordered, and when you order something you obviously pay for it. You paid for it, so you're expecting what you paid for. When you and I make *duʿāʾ*, we pay nothing. We pay *nothing*. When you pay nothing, then you have no expectations, you have no right to complain about what you get. You don't get to say, 'Hey! Wait, I asked for a hundred on my exam. I made *duʿāʾ* last night. I still got a forty. What is this Allah? I placed the right order!' You and I don't get to do that. Allah is not here to serve you and me as customers.

We're used to customer service in this world. We are used to it so much that we think the way we are going to deal with Allah, is the same. Some of the young people today; unfortunately, their relationship with their parents has become like their parents are supposed to provide them customer service. 'Mum, I asked you to buy me Grand Theft Auto! How come you didn't get it yet?', 'I told you I'm going to do my homework!' Like your homework is payment or something, right? Because we feel so entitled all the time, we bring this entitled attitude when we turn to Allah and we make *du'ā'* to Him. '*Yā Allāh*, heal me.' '*Yā Allāh*, get me a promotion.' '*Yā Allāh*, do this for me or do that for me.' And it doesn't happen; and you're like: 'Forget this, I don't need prayer. I even took the time out to pray and He didn't give!'

One of the first things we need to understand that when he made *du'ā'*, *Zakariyyā* (*'alayhi al-salām*) said: *wa-lam akun bi-du'āika Rabbi shaqiyyā*—he mentioned the word *Rabb*. Why? He said 'Master! You're the Master. I'm the slave. You are the ultimately high'. There's no position higher than *Rabb*, than master, in any language. Master is the highest you can be; and when you have a master, that makes you a slave. Nobody has a worse job than a slave; there is no status lower than that. So you and I are of the lowest status and Allah is of the highest status. And from that position when you ask; you're not in a position to be placing orders. We're in a position of humility. Master whatever you give. Master whatever you give, I'll take it. And if you decide not to give, I accept, because you know better than I do.

Mūsā (*'alayhi al-salām*) is homeless. He is a fugitive from the law, because he was wanted for murder, and he is sitting under a tree, and he says: *Rabbi innī limā anzalta ilayya min khayrin faqīr* (*al-Qaṣaṣ* 28: 24)—Master, whatever you send me, I'll take it. I'm not going to be picky. He's got no food, he's got no clothes, he's got no home. So if some food comes to him. Some rice comes to him, 'Oh, actually I'm on a diet. I need some salad and I need some…'. No, no, no. Whatever comes to him, he'll take it. When a job comes to him he's not going to say, 'Actually I'm a pretty qualified guy. I need a job that's equivalent to my qualifications. If you're going to give me a job that's beneath my status, no thank you'. No, he's not going to do that because he begged Allah, whatever you give me I'll take it.

So now *Zakariyyā* (*'alayhi al-salām*) said, 'I've never been miserable, I've never been depressed, I've never rushed'. By the way, in the word *shiqwah* is also the meaning of 'rushing'. They say when people give up in the war and they run, that's also called *mushāqāt* in Arabic, from the same linguistic root. You know what that means? There are some people that make *du'ā'* and they expect the results when? Quickly! Give it to me now! Express delivery! Let's see this *du'ā'* come to life! Let it happen! And when it doesn't happen: 'Forget it, who needs *du'ā'* anyway'. *Subḥān Allāh*!

The last thing I want to share with you about this word *shiqwah*—before I go to *Ibrāhīm* (*'alayhi al-salām*) —about this attitude of being miserable. There are people who come before Allah (*ʿazza wa-jall*) on the day of judgement and they say:

قَالُوا۟ رَبَّنَا غَلَبَتْ عَلَيْنَا شِقْوَتُنَا وَكُنَّا قَوْمًا ضَآلِّينَ ﴿١٠٦﴾
(المؤمنون ٢٣ : ١٠٦)

They will say: "Our Lord! Our misfortune prevailed over us. We were indeed an erring people".
(Al-Mu'minūn 23: 106)

They come on Judgement Day; they're about to go into the bad place, and they give their reasons. They were believers and they did not make it to *jannah*. Why not? They explain themselves: our depression, our misery, and our negative attitudes towards you; they overtook us—*ghalabat ʿalaynā*. This attitude we had towards you, this frustration we had with you, *yā Allāh*, was so heavy that we could never think of you in a good way. We did not have good expectations from you and it overwhelmed us; and it made us miserable, wretched people overall.

Today, interesting things are happening in the world and one of the interesting things is that among young people, there is a rise in atheism. There is a rise in young people that don't believe in God, and it's actually rising all over the world. It's not just an American phenomenon it's happening in Europe, it's happening in Asia, in Africa, all over. There are statistics about this. And it's interesting if you look at the lives of leading atheists—many of them who lived in recent times—some of them died of overdoses in drugs and had suffered from serious depression. When they turn their backs on Allah then all that's left is misery. Really all that's left is a dark, dark life. And so *duʿā'*, when you don't have the right attitude, it might even lead you away from Allah Himself. What is between this Master of ours and us? The thing that ties us together, the thing that gives us a relationship is actually *duʿā'*, itself.

Now moving along, *Ibrāhīm* (*ʿalayhi al-salām*) when he was leaving his family because his father and the entire village was worshipping idols he said:

وَأَعْتَزِلُكُمْ وَمَا تَدْعُونَ مِن دُونِ ٱللَّهِ وَأَدْعُواْ رَبِّى عَسَىٰٓ أَلَّآ أَكُونَ بِدُعَآءِ رَبِّى شَقِيًّا ﴿٤٨﴾

(مريم ١٩ : ٤٨)

> "I shall withdraw from you and all that you call upon beside Allah. I shall only call upon my Lord. I trust the prayer to my Lord will not go unanswered."
>
> (Maryam 19: 48)

He said: I'm leaving all of you; I'm leaving all the things you worship other than Allah too and I am calling on my Master, I'm making *duʿā'* to Him. And then he said something really profound. It's the same surah, *Sūrat Maryam*. He said: hopefully, I will not be miserable when I make *duʿāʾ* to my master. He added the word 'hopefully'—*ʿasā*—Why? *Zakariyyā* did not say hopefully. He said I have never been but *Zakariyyā* (*ʿalayhi al-salām*) was talking about the past—I have never been depressed, when I pray to you. And *Ibrahim* (*ʿalayhi al-salām*) is humble about his future. He says hopefully I can maintain my *īmān*. 'Hopefully there will never come a time when I pray to you, *yā Allāh*, and I am not filled with hope. I hope I never do that.' So he is actually humble, he is not self-righteous and thinks I will never, ever do that. I am always going to be righteous; I am always going to make *duʿāʾ* the right way. His humility is suggested in the word *ʿasā*.

And now finally, like I said, people come to me and say: what am I supposed to think? My *duʿāʾ* didn't get answered, I've been praying so hard. Allah is not answering my prayers! How are we supposed to think about this stuff? First of all, acknowledge that Allah is providing not just for you, He is providing for all of creation. He is providing for the believer and He is also providing for the disbeliever. They get jobs too, they have children too, they have happiness too, they have food on their tables too, they get promotions too, they get sick also and they get healed. So the people of *duʿāʾ* have trouble in this world and the people without *duʿāʾ* also have trouble and challenges in this world and Allah does not just give gifts and blessings in this world to believers He also gives them to disbelievers and *kuffār* and the worst people. He gives and He gives and He gives and He decides when to give—*wa-Llāh yaqbiḍ wa-yabsuṭ* (*al-Baqarah* 2: 245)—Allah takes and Allah gives; Allah pulls back a little, He constrains your budget a little, He takes away the health a little, He'll give you some difficulty sometimes and sometimes He will let the difficulty go. That's up to Allah (*ʿazza wa-jall*), but then what's the point of *duʿā'* if Allah provides everyone anyway?

The point of *duʿā'* is actually to acknowledge before Allah, it's an admission to Allah that He provides and we are in need. The *mu'min*, the believer in the time of *Āl Firʿawn* (Pharaoh's dynasty), he said it best; the attitude of *duʿā'* is captured in one phrase—*wa-ufawwiḍ amrī ilā Allāh* (*Ghāfir* 40: 44)—that's what *duʿā'* is at the end of the day. Let me explain what that means: *al-tafwīḍ* in Arabic actually means to leave something in somebody else's hands i.e.—*jaʿala al-ākhar al-ḥākim fī amrihi*—he put somebody else in charge of his matter, that's called *tafwīḍ*. And interestingly in old Arabic they say—*baynī wa-baynahū fawḍah*—and *fawḍah* has the same root. It actually means I have a partnership with this guy. In other words when I leave the matter to Allah, Allah is as worried about this, if not more, than I am. Allah is not some other that I am asking; Allah is sharing with me in this matter. Allah is actually a part of this situation. Whatever I am feeling, Allah knows better than even I know. If I care about something, I should know that I have made *tafwīḍ* of Allah, which means not only do I trust Allah with whatever He does, I know Allah cares about what I am asking Him. It's not like He doesn't care. Nobody gets to say Allah doesn't care just because Allah doesn't answer the way you and I expected.

Part of this is our *īmān* in the names of Allah and this is what I want to conclude on. The angels said: *lā ʿilm lanā illā mā ʿallamtanā* (*al-Baqarah* 2: 245)—Master we have no knowledge, whatsoever, except what you taught us. One of the names of Allah is *al-ʿAlīm*—the one who knows everything. Now, you and I think we know; Allah actually knows. There is a difference. Allah says He brings you out: *min buṭūn ummahātikum lā taʿlamūn shay'an* (*al-Naḥl* 16: 78)—from the bellies of your mothers. He said He brought you out of the bellies of your mothers, you still don't know anything. He didn't say He brought you out of the bellies of your mothers, you *didn't* know anything—since a baby actually doesn't know anything. Rather, He says I brought you out of your mothers and, by the way, you still don't know anything—*subḥān Allāh. Wa-Llāh yaʿlam wa-antum lā taʿlamūn*—Allah in fact, knows. This is part of our *īmān*—Allah knows and I don't know.

Let's put that to the test. I think I know what's best, but Allah actually knows what's best. I think that getting better is best. I think that getting that job is the best.

I think that this difficulty if I can get out of it, it's the best. But Allah knows, way better than I know. He knows way better than I know. I make *du'ā'* based on what I think is best—that's what I can do as a human being. I will only ask Allah based on the limited knowledge that I have, but thankfully Allah knows better than you and me and everybody else so He will answer based on perfect knowledge. And maybe the best thing for you is that He does not answer right away, that He does not give you what you are asking for right away.

One of the most incredible examples of that in Islamic history, I call it Islamic history because all prophets are from Islam, is the *ḥawāriyyūn* of *'Īsā* (*'alayhi al-salām*).

رَبَّنَآ ءَامَنَّا بِمَآ أَنزَلْتَ وَٱتَّبَعْنَا ٱلرَّسُولَ فَٱكْتُبْنَا مَعَ ٱلشَّـٰهِدِينَ ۝٥٣
(آل عمران ٣: ٥٣)

> "Our Lord! We believe in the commandment You have revealed and we obey the Messenger; make us, then, one of those who bear witness (to the Truth)."
>
> (Āl 'Imrān 3: 53)

They made *du'ā'* to Allah: *Rabbanā innanā āmannā wa-ttaba'nā al-Rasūl fa-ktubnā ma'a al-shāhidīn.* We've come to *īmān*, we're following the messenger *'Īsā* (*'alayhi al-salām*) write us among those who are witnesses. And *'Īsā* (*'alayhi al-salām*) clearly needed help:

... قَالَ عِيسَى ٱبۡنُ مَرۡيَمَ لِلۡحَوَارِيِّـۧنَ مَنۡ أَنصَارِيٓ إِلَى ٱللَّهِۖ قَالَ ٱلۡحَوَارِيُّونَ نَحۡنُ أَنصَارُ ٱللَّهِۖ ... ﴿١٤﴾

(الصف ٦١ : ١٤)

... as Jesus, son of Mary, said to the disciples: "Who is my helper in (calling people) to Allah?" The disciples had responded by saying: "We are Allah's helpers"...

(Al-Ṣaff 61: 14)

He said: who's going to aid me towards Allah? *Qāl al-ḥawāriyyūn naḥnu anṣār Allāh*—They said we're going to help you in the cause of Allah. We're going to be the aides of Allah. Now Allah in that *āyah* said *fa-ayyadnā alladhīna āmanū 'alā 'aduwwihim*—We aided those who believed, We gave them help against their enemies. Allah says about the followers of *'Īsā* (*'alayhi al-salām*)—think carefully about this last part—Allah says We gave them help against their enemies. But you know historically that the people who believed in *tawhīd*, followers of *'Īsā* (*'alayhi al-salām*) were pretty much annihilated and a lot of them didn't even make a comeback until centuries after. In other words, Allah did aid them but in His own way. It's not on your terms; it's not on my terms.

Ibrahim (*'alayhi al-salām*) made *du'ā'* that a child from my generation should be raised who will recite the Qur'an, who will recite the *āyāt* of Allah: *yatlū 'alayhim ayātik wa-yu'allimuhum al-kitāb wa-l-ḥikmah wa-yuzakkīhim* (*al-Baqarah* 2: 129). He made *duʿā'*. It's a very sincere *duʿā'*. But that child was not Ismāʿīl (*ʿalayhi al-salām*), nor Ismāʿīl's child, nor his grandchild, nor his grandchild's grandchild. Many generations later the *duʿā'* of *Ibrahim* (*ʿalayhi al-salām*) is fulfilled when Allah knows is the best time. At that time Muhammad (*ṣallā Allāh ʿalayhi wa-sallam*) is born; then at the age of forty he is given revelation. Because Allah decides what is best. He knows and you and I don't know. The thing we have to remember in making *duʿā'* is: first of all, we're not in a position to place orders. Secondly: whatever I'm asking for *yā Allāh*, if this is good for me, give me and if not, I trust your decision. Don't think that your situation is unique; every situation you and I go through is mentioned in one way or the other in the Qur'an.

Those of you that are sick—*innī massanī al-ḍurr wa-anta arḥam al-raḥimīn* (*al-Anbiyā'* 21: 83)—the *duʿā'* is already there. *Ayyūb* (*ʿalayhi al-salām*) turns to Allah and says, '*Yā Allāh*, the pain is getting to me' he doesn't even ask, '*Yā Allāh*, cure me', because he doesn't know if that is the best thing. He just turns to Allah and says: '*Yā Allāh*, there is no one who shows more love and more mercy and more care than you. I already know that. My pain has not shaken my belief; my pain does not shake my faith.' Most people when they feel a little discomfort their faith is shaken. I pray that Allah makes us real people of *duʿā'*, real people of *tawakkul*. I pray Allah does not make us of those who give up on Allah quickly. That our *du'ās* to Allah bring us closer and closer to Him and make us of those whom Allah gives strength of *īmān* through their prayers. That if Allah does not provide what you are hoping for immediately, you learn to say to yourself that definitely whatever Allah has planned for me in the circumstance that I am in, is absolutely better for me. This is the test of this life.

Stop asking yourself what did I do to deserve this? Stop asking yourself that question. Allah does not hate you, Allah did not abandon you. He doesn't abandon His creation; He loves His creation. He created us after all and He made us in this beautiful way. All the good experiences you have in your life, all the love you enjoy in your life, all the beautiful children we see in our families they are a gift from Allah. They are not our making. They are a gift from Allah because He loves us all. The things that are around you, if you learned to appreciate them then your attitude towards Allah will change. You wouldn't be people of complaint anymore. So I remind myself and you that the attitude, I deserve better, is not a good attitude. It's not a healthy attitude. Allah knows what we deserve. As a matter of fact we start with the assumption that you and I deserve nothing. The slave deserves nothing; the Master gives anyway. He gives gifts so everything we do have is a gift of Allah (*'azza wa-jall*). May Allah (*'azza wa-jall*) make us a people of gratitude, make us a people of *tawakkul* and make us a people of sincere, accepted *du'ā'*.

PART II

CREATING A COHESIVE MUSLIM COMMUNITY

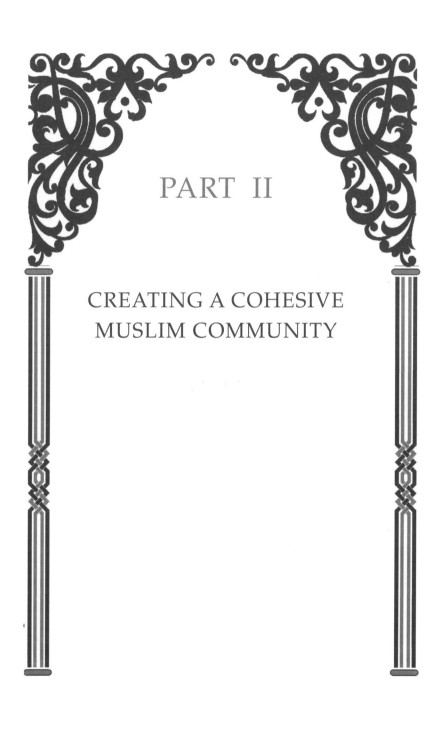

CHAPTER 3

Criticism

In this reminder, *in shā' Allāh* I just want to share with you one small section, from a very small surah. *Sūrat al-ʿAṣr* is probably a surah you have heard many, many talks on, many reminders on; and it is important we remind ourselves of the wisdom that's encapsulated inside this very beautiful surah. In one sense, it's a summary of the entire Qur'an; you can say it is a summary of the entire religion of Islam. All we have to do to succeed in this life, or more accurately all we have to do to avoid failure in this life, is described in *Sūrat al-ʿAṣr*.

Many times when I give *durūs* on *Sūrat al-ʿAṣr*, I let people know in the beginning, and I'll let you know too, that *Sūrat al-ʿAṣr* is not about attaining success. It's not a surah that teaches Muslims how to become successful; it actually teaches Muslims how not to become failures. There are teachers, when they start a course they give advice: here's what you do to get an A, here's how you get a hundred on the test, here's how you become the top student; that's one kind of advice. And that is there in the Qur'an too. But then there are other teachers or there are other times and the teacher says, 'Okay, you have to meet these minimum requirements; and if you don't meet these minimum requirements, you fail. Forget about the A, I won't even give you a D, you're going to get an F. You're not passing this class'.

Sūrat al-ʿAṣr is about that minimum. It's an urgency for us to remind ourselves of that minimum because it's important to remind ourselves not just of the higher grades and the extra credit assignments that will give us more and more promotions in this religion; none of that is relevant if you're not even passing. None of that makes sense if you're not even meeting the minimum requirements, right?

So this reminder is not about *Sūrat al-ʿAṣr* itself, as I stated in the beginning, it's about one piece of it that easily gets neglected. There is one piece of it that we have to pay extra attention to because Allah (*ʿazza wa-jall*) put four connected conditions on meeting the minimum requirements:

1. *Illā alladhīna āmanū*
2. *Wa-ʿamilū al-ṣāliḥāt*
3. *Wa-tawāṣaw bi-l-ḥaqq*
4. *Wa-tawāṣaw bi-l-ṣabr.*

There are four conditions and in this reminder,

more than anything else, I wanted to focus on just one condition. And it's not *illā alladhīna āmanū*, and it's not *wa-ʿamilū al-ṣāliḥāt*. In this reminder, I wanted to reflect a little bit with you about the idea that Allah captures inside the phrase: *wa-tawāṣaw bi-l-ḥaqq*.

I think it's important to take advantage of short surahs and give reminders on them and discuss them more because pretty much every Muslim either knows them already, even our children know them already, and if you don't, it wouldn't take you much to memorize them. So it wouldn't take much to remind ourselves of the lessons that are captured and the wisdom that is buried inside these words, *subḥān Allāh*.

So first a rough translation of the surah is in order:

وَٱلْعَصْرِ ۝١ إِنَّ ٱلْإِنسَـٰنَ لَفِى خُسْرٍ ۝٢ إِلَّا ٱلَّذِينَ ءَامَنُوا۟ وَعَمِلُوا۟ ٱلصَّـٰلِحَـٰتِ وَتَوَاصَوْا۟ بِٱلْحَقِّ وَتَوَاصَوْا۟ بِٱلصَّبْرِ ۝٣

(العصر ١٠٣ : ١-٣)

> By the time! Lo! Man is in a state of loss; save those who have faith and do righteous deeds, and counsel each other to hold on to truth and counsel each other to be steadfast.
>
> (Al-ʿAṣr 103: 1-3)

In the surah, Allah swears by the time that's running out, that no doubt every single human being is drowning in loss, in some loss. And then Allah says the only exception are those who've believed—*illā alladhīna āmanū wa-ʿamilū al-ṣāliḥāt*—and they do the few good deeds that are asked of them. *Wa-tawāṣaw bi-l-ḥaqq* is commonly translated: 'and they enjoin the truth'. Some more contemporary translations try to suggest, they encourage each other towards the truth. These are the kinds of translations you get for *wa-tawāṣaw bi-l-ḥaqq*. Similarly for *wa-tawāṣaw bi-l-ṣabr*: they enjoin perseverance, they encourage each other to be patient.

I wanted to dig a little bit first into this phrase—*wa-tawāṣaw bi-l-ḥaqq*—to give us a perspective on what Allah is saying in this incredible surah. But before I do that, I want some perspective of what is motivating me to reflect on this surah. We are living today in a culture that thrives on criticism. People go to see a movie and they give it two stars or three stars or four stars, they like to give a critique to it. People watch a YouTube video and they like to comment and present their criticisms in that comment. People post something on Facebook and others comment and critique and offer their counter opinion like the Arabic saying goes: *li-kulli khiṭāb jawāb*—every time somebody voices an opinion, somebody's got something counter to say. There's always a counter argument, criticism, evaluation—'I kinda like it', 'I agree but I don't agree with this thing or that thing', 'it's okay', 'it's not great', etc. So we're used to that kind of culture. That's the consumer culture we're in, you can't even just go shopping. Actually when you go shopping you look at the criticisms of the product first. You Google trouble with this computer or trouble with this car or whatever and then you find out what those ratings are. When you go buy something on Amazon, you look at the star ratings or customer reviews first.

So we're in the mode, we're surrounded by this idea of constant, constant criticism. And it's not just about being consumers, it's become a part of our culture. So now we love criticizing teachers, students, parents, children, co-workers, bosses, managers, friends, speakers, audiences. It doesn't matter who. The imam might be complaining about the congregation, the congregation might be complaining about the imam. Friends are complaining about each other, usually not in each other's presence. People complain about Islamic organizations, Islamic organizations complain about other Islamic organizations, it's just become a thing. We don't even think twice about it. As a matter of fact, when I travel and meet people from different communities, I don't know anything about them, I only spend a couple of hours, maybe a day with those people; they're taking me from the airport so I say 'How's your community?' They say, '*Mā shā' Allāh*, it's good but we've got a lot of problems'. And then there is a list of twenty criticisms. So it began with *mā shā' Allāh* and *al-ḥamd li-Llāh*, but we're programmed to almost constantly think about criticisms. If you look at the kinds of comments, the kinds of communications that are especially public nowadays because of social media but even in regular TV media and even in our common discourse; most of the time what we are talking about is criticism. Much of what we talk about is critical. And sometimes people hide behind the defence, 'Well, I'm being constructively critical'. I'm criticizing to improve things. Now, here's the thing with that. And that's what I really wanted to highlight here. This surah is actually giving us a pretty important principle about criticism. It's included in the surah but many don't pay attention to that idea.

So let's think a little bit about this wording, the word *tawāṣaw* comes from the original word *al-waṣiyyah*, in the Arabic language. The word *waṣiyyah* is used when you leave a will. When somebody is dying and they leave parting advice. For example, some elderly person's on their deathbed and their children and their grandchildren are surrounding them, before the *rūḥ* leaves the body, the few words they say could be called a *waṣiyyah*. Everybody around them is crying, they're trying to listen to every last word they say because this might be the last time they hear that voice. Those words are going to ring in their head the rest of their lives—that's a *waṣiyyah*. And by the way, *waṣiyyah* is related to *wirāthah*—*wirāthah* is leaving a will, right?

In the Qur'an Allah (*ʿazza wa-jall*) even says:

dhālikum waṣṣākum bihi (*al-Anʿām* 6: 151)—that is how Allah gives you advice. In other words when somebody's about to die or they know they are terminally ill or they are about to leave and they're not sure if they are going to come back. Then what do they do? They call their loved ones together and they say listen, 'I may or may not see you again but I really want you to listen to my advice please. End the fight with your brother, be good to your mother, do this, do that'—they give some advice. That kind of advice is called *waṣiyyah*. And *waṣiyyah*, therefore, is never technically, given to strangers. You don't give *waṣiyyah* to strangers. You actually give *waṣiyyah* to loved ones, by definition. We haven't even gotten into the linguistics yet, this is just a social reality.

Waṣiyyah is not technically given to strangers, it is given to people you care about, people that love you, people that are sad that you are leaving them and so there is a sense of urgency to want to hear what you have to say. They are going to drop everything; they are not going to be texting while you are giving the *waṣiyyah*. They are not going to be on the phone like: 'Yeah I'm listening to both of you'. No, No, No. They're not going to do that. They're not going to have the TV on, they are going to give you one hundred per cent attention because you're about to give them a *waṣiyyah*. And it's one of the most powerful memories in people's lives; some people have had that trauma in their life. They've had a loved one pass away, they've been next to the loved one that passed away and they remember the words that were said. They remember those parting words; they stay in their head for the rest of their lives.

Now that's important, that's one dimension of *waṣiyyah* that I wanted to highlight first. There are other dimensions that I'll highlight but I wanted to start with this one. Why? Because when Allah says, and we translate, 'They enjoin each other to the truth', then we're missing one fundamental reality. To tell somebody about the truth, in keeping with the word *waṣiyyah*, you have to love the one you're telling. You have to have love for the one you are telling some truth to. A lot of times when we criticize, we criticize under the banner of truth, 'I'm just speaking the truth brother'. But do you love the one you're speaking the truth about? Because if they're a believer, and you disagree with the other believer; we disagree with each other all the time, that's fine. But is your criticism, even if it is criticism, is it first and foremost rooted in love? In concern? Do you care about them? And is that what's driving you to give this *waṣiyyah*?

Then there is the other matter, sometimes we are afraid to criticize—that's the opposite problem. On the one hand we're overly critical and on the other hand we are not critical at all. In other words we don't want to speak out and say the right thing because somebody might get upset. 'I don't want to say anything, I know my uncle has a really bad temper and he yells at his kids and he yells at his wife, but he's an elder. So I shouldn't say anything.' Or there's one of your relatives and they do a lot of backbiting. Every time you see them, they're talking bad about somebody else—'I shouldn't say anything, I don't know, they'll feel bad if I say something'. So you hold back from saying something; but actually part of your love for them is that you're honest to them. This is something Muslims have to learn, it's very hard, you know what we do? The way we show love to our loved ones is we don't tell them the truth. 'Er, their feelings might get hurt.' That's not love. That's deception.

You're not doing them a favour by not bringing something important to their attention. You're not doing them a favour by allowing them to do more wrong that is being written against them. It's being reported, it's not like they are getting away with it. If you love them, you don't want them to get into more trouble. You want to help them, but you know what? The tone that you're going to take and I'm going to take; the time I will pick to give the advice; the sentiments with which I will carry it; the words I'm going to choose—all of them will be governed by the love I have for them. And if love is not there, if that concern is not there, then we are going to pick some pretty offensive ways of saying things.

Your uncle has a temper problem and you walk up to him, 'By the way I read a reminder today, Uncle, and you have a real temper problem. You have a serious issue. I just wanted to fulfil my obligation to *Sūrat al-ʿAṣr* and let you know. *Al-salām ʿalaykum*', and you walk away. No, No, No. You have to become loving and creative in trying to bring something to others—this is part of *tawāṣī*. 'Uncle, I was wondering… I don't want you to be upset or anything but I noticed your son was really sad the other day. Were you angry with him?' 'Yeah, well, you know.' And then you're like, 'Uncle, I know you get angry, I know he does the wrong thing but can you be just a little bit easier because he is really depressed; and he cares and he doesn't want to disappoint you'.

You find a softer way of saying the same thing. You're not so direct and aggressive, you still said the truth but because it's coupled with the idea of *tawāṣī*, of *waṣiyyah*—it's soft, it's loving. And by the way the other thing about *waṣiyyah* is, when *waṣiyyah* is given, it goes right to the heart of the other. *Waṣiyyah* is given to the loved one whose heart is softened, he is already in tears and that's when you give *waṣiyyah*. You have to find a way to emotionally reach someone. Sometimes when you give advice, you know what happens? People become more aggressive. And even worse off than they were before you gave them advice, just because of the *way* you gave advice. Just because of the way you talked to them, they've become worse. So you're not making things better—'I'm enjoining the truth brother!' You might be enjoining the truth but you're not doing *tawāṣī bi-l-ḥaqq*. Those are two different things; maybe you got caught up in the English translation or something. That's not *tawāṣaw bi-l-ḥaqq*. So that's one dimension.

The other dimension of this word that, *subḥān Allāh,* is so beautiful is that the verb *waṣiyyah*. They in Arabic—*waṣiyat al-'arḍ: iṭṭaṣal al-nabāt bihā*—when the vegetation on the earth like grass and trees they have deep roots and it's hard to pluck them out. Sometimes the earth has weak grass and shrubs and things like that, when the wind blows, they blow away. Other times the earth has plants that are deeply rooted and connected and can't be separated easily; that is part of the meaning of the root of the word *waṣiyyah*. When the earth is bonded together with its plant life. The implication of that in the word *tawāṣaw* is that they stay together with each other.

Now when you're giving somebody truth, obviously they're doing something wrong and you're telling them the truth; or maybe they're falling behind and you're giving them advice. This means that this might create friction but Allah embedded inside the language of the word that you have to stick with loved ones. You can't have one harsh conversation and give up on them. You can't try to give somebody advice and they blow up in your face and you're like, 'Forget that, I'm not talking to them again', 'I hate my cousin. It's over. He's got a temper problem'. No, no, no. *Tawāṣaw* actually means they stay together with each other for the purpose of committing to the truth. You can't give up on family, you can't give up on friends and you can't give up on other believers. The *āyah* didn't begin with families; it began with: *illā alladhīna āmanū wa-ʿamilū al-ṣāliḥāt*. None of us gives up on the other one. None of us says about the other one 'They're a lost cause'; and, by the way, this idea of *tawāṣī bi-l-ḥaqq*; this is actually the building block of the Muslim community.

In a Muslim community sometimes there are people who make mistakes. People that we know, in our community, we find out that they made a mistake. They did something bad, they lost their temper, they said something they shouldn't have said, they sent an email they shouldn't have sent or whatever, and they are now, forever villains. 'This guy man. Remember his email from 1998. We cannot have him. He's here again, oh, watch it!' No, no, no. You don't give up on your people. Even if they made a mistake, you don't give up. This is part of *tawāṣī bi-l-ḥaqq*. You have to stick together. They say in Arabic: *al-waṣiyy: jara'id al-nakhl allatī yuḥzam bihā*—the bark of the palm tree has a certain paper-like substance that comes out of it. They bind it together and make a rope out of it that you can tie something with. That's from the word *waṣiyyah* also, meaning you're tied to each other because of the truth. The *bā'* here could be *bā' al-sababiyyah. Wa-tawāṣaw bi-l-ḥaqq* could mean: you are bonded to each other because of your commitment to the truth. This is the quality of the people who don't fail. You know what Allah is telling us? If we don't do this, we have failed. This is the minimum, this is not a higher expectation; this is a minimum requirement of *tawāṣī bi-l-ḥaqq*. We have to stick with one another.

Now another couple of things before I conclude. Another dimension of the phrase *tawāṣaw* in *wa-tawāṣaw bi-l-ḥaqq*. Some students reading this, who are learning Arabic, know the pattern in *ṣarf*: *tafāʿala*. *Tafāʿala* is used when two parties, two sides or more, are doing the same thing and they are co-operating with each other. In other words, I'm giving you advice and you are giving me advice. You are letting my advice get into your heart and I am ready to let your advice get into my heart. That is *tawāṣī*—like *tashāruk, taʿāwun, taḥāwur*—anything in that pattern of the Arabic language, there are two parties that are both equally engaged in something.

Now, what happens in our families and by extension our communities is there are some people who are professional advice givers. Their job is to give the advice and boy they get really offended if you were to give them advice. Bad idea! 'Wait you're going to give me advice?! I'm the *khaṭīb*, I give. See the mic—it's on my collar. You don't have a mic on. You're not giving me advice, I give you advice brother!' It's not just about a *khaṭīb*, or an *ʿālim*, or a speaker. It could be an elder in the family, it could be the CEO of a company, it could be a physician—I'm not picking on doctors—but I'm saying that you're used to giving patients advice, you're used to giving the nurses advice, you're used to giving the administration advice; then somebody at the masjid gives you advice and you're like, 'Excuse me!' You're not used to taking advice; you're used to giving it. Part of *tawāṣī* is that the people you give advice to, the same people I give advice to, are the same people I am willing to take advice from.

Now that's hard! That's hard, because sometimes we give our wife advice but then the wife decides she is going to give us some advice back. That doesn't go so well, you know. We like the one-way street, this two-way street thing is: 'Hey, Hey! Wait a second!' Sometimes we like to give young people advice but sometimes when they say, 'Uncle you know, maybe if we did things this way' and they try to give us advice we are like, 'Know your role, don't try to get too big for your shoes'. We put them in their place, what's the idea behind that? That's not *tawāṣī*. *Tawāṣī* means I am as willing and as concerned for the other to give me loving counsel. My love for them, has softened me towards them, so even when they ask something of me, legitimate or illegitimate, I am willing to listen; I am willing to listen patiently. I am not going to reject it just because they are saying it.

I'm reminded of a really beautiful incident in the life of Umar (*raḍiya Allāh ʿanhu*) on the matter of *tawāṣī*, being able to not just give advice, but to take it. At the time he's *Amīr al-Mu'minīn*, his job is to give the *khuṭbah*, his job is to advise people on what to do and to remind them about honesty. He was on one of his strolls and he happened to peer through a window. He sees a guy drinking and he looks like he is drunk. Now, Umar (*raḍiya Allāh ʿanhu*), you know his temper! He busts down the door, grabs the guy by the collar, 'You drinking under my watch!?' The guy says, 'I did one haram act, you did three haram acts'. Umar's (*raḍiya Allāh ʿanhu*) like what? What are you talking about? He says first of all you looked inside my window. You're supposed to observe the privacy of a Muslim. You're not supposed to look inside. Second, you made the assumption that I'm drinking alcohol. You couldn't have known. I could have been drinking water. I could have been drinking milk; you shouldn't be making assumptions about Muslims. Third, you entered my home without permission, you're not supposed to. Until you are wanted, don't go into a believer's house. You did three haram acts! Umar (*raḍiya Allāh ʿanhu*) apologized, let him go and walked away.

He's the head of the state, he could have said, 'Oh oh, you got a mouth too, huh?' 'You come with me I'll give you special treatment'. No, no, no. He left. A few weeks go by and Umar (*raḍiya Allāh ʿanhu*) is giving the *khuṭbah* and this guy walks into the masjid, same guy. Umar ends the *khuṭbah* and he calls the guy over and privately says to him, 'Hey, ever since then, I never told anything about you'; and the guy says to Umar (*raḍiya Allāh ʿanhu*), 'Ever since then, I stopped drinking'—that's *tawāṣī*. Even though he is in a position of leadership, he is willing to listen. He is not going to dismiss somebody, even the guy who's drunk, Umar (*raḍiya Allāh ʿanhu*) is taking advice from a guy who smells of alcohol. They understood what *tawāṣī bi-l-ḥaqq* means.

As I near the conclusion, I want to highlight some more things about *tawāṣī bi-l-ḥaqq*. What does it mean for you and me to live by it? One dimension is the *bā'*, when you say *bi-l-ḥaqq*, it can actually be looked at in multiple ways; it can be looked at as a *mafʿūl bihi*, or it can be looked at as a *ḥāl*. What that means in simple English is, when you give somebody counsel be honest in your counsel. Be sincere in your counsel, no strings attached. I am not giving you advice because it will benefit me in some way. I'm not giving you counsel because I've got some other agenda that will support something that I'm looking to get done. I am only giving you advice because I care about you. My motives are pure. I am truthful in the way that I give you counsel, that is a condition.

So sometimes we only give advice to people that, if we don't give them that advice, the business will get hurt; or if we don't give them that advice some of our other relationships might get messed up—there's some other agenda. There is something else tied to this advice, otherwise you don't care. Otherwise you would never call this person. You only call them because calling them has some benefit to yourself. That isn't *tawāṣī bi-l-ḥaqq*. *Tawāṣī bi-l-ḥaqq* is you call people, you follow up with them, you ask them questions—when you actually care about them. Now here's for example a situation just to put this in practical terms. You have a friend but you never call him. You know he is going through a divorce, you know he's going through some trouble; but you never call him, you don't care. Then you found out that he has something of yours or he has some contact that you need. He has a phone number for somebody; you need that phone number, so now you call him. 'How's it going? How's your situation? Any better? By the way I need a phone number.' You don't really care about his situation, all you care about is your phone number. That's not *tawāṣī bi-l-ḥaqq. Tawāṣī bi-l-ḥaqq* is when you call someone because you care. Not because of some other reason, that's part of the sincerity inside the words *bi-l-ḥaqq*.

And finally, the last bit in *tawāṣī bi-l-ḥaqq*, if you look at it as a *maf'ūl*, then it means: 'using the truth they advise each other'. In other words, a lot of *Ṣaḥābah* interpreted *al-ḥaqq* here as *al-Qur'ān*, i.e. *tawāṣī bi-l-Qur'ān*. In other words, they advise each other with the ultimate truth. They don't beat around the bush. Part of fixing our relationships, all of our friendships, family relationships, your relationship with your parents, your relationship with your children, part of that is honesty. There are so many people who don't honestly tell their parents that they're being hurt. They don't honestly tell their children that their words are hurting them. They don't honestly tell their husband or their wife how they truly feel, they're not honest about it. And you know why they don't say it, because they say well if I'm honest then it might create a fight. If I tell people how I really feel, they might get really angry at me. Let me tell you, when you keep bottling your emotions up, that's not *ṣabr*. You're collecting more gunpowder and eventually it will explode. Eventually it's all going to come out and it's going to get really ugly.

We have to get in the habit of being honest with

each other in our relationships—using the truth in our relationships—yet at the same time maintaining a demeanour of love and respect. Maintaining a demeanour of concern for the other. I am equally concerned for my mother as I am for myself. Some of you sons reading this today, your mothers want you to get married to someone you don't want to get married to, for example. And you're like, 'I shouldn't say anything, it's my mum, and I shouldn't say anything'. Actually you should, but lovingly. 'Mum, I don't like her. I love you; you can beat me, here's a shoe. Just beat me, but I don't like her. I can't do it.' And girls the same way, you have to speak up. It doesn't mean, 'I'm NOT going to do it mum, you DON'T UNDERSTAND ME!'. No, no. That's not *tawāṣī* either, you have to keep a loving demeanour. You have to keep a respectful demeanour, but that doesn't mean you shy away from saying the truth. That is what is necessary in all of our relationships.

If we can learn to do that in our families then we can slowly learn to do that at the level of community. Then we can become people that can take criticism because we are not giving criticism in a nasty, ugly, mean way; in an insensitive way. We are doing it because we have already developed a kind of bond with each other where we can speak honestly with each other. We can have criticism going back and forth with each other and it's fine. All human beings recognize that they make mistakes. The only way they grow is if they learn from one another, *subḥān Allāh*.

So I pray that Allah (*'azza wa-jall*) helps us fulfil this beautiful, simple and yet comprehensive advice of *tawāṣī bi-l-ḥaqq*. O Allah, make us of those who believe (*alladhīna āmanū*), do righteous deeds (*wa-'amilū al-ṣāliḥāt*), and are people of *tawāṣī bi-l-ḥaqq* and *tawāṣī bi-l-ṣabr*. Āmīn!

CHAPTER 4

Assumptions

In *Sūrat al-Ḥujurāt*, the forty-nineth surah, there is a list of timeless Muslim morals, Muslim principles that, if we abide by them, teach us how to live together as a healthy society. These principles aren't just about how Muslims are supposed to treat each other but also about the way we deal with all of humanity. How we're supposed to be with the people around us. Each one of them is probably the subject of a reminder on its own, which is why instead of giving you the entire list and walking you through all of those principles, *in shā' Allāh taʿālā* I encourage you to read and think about them on your own. Surah forty-nine from beginning to end; just ponder the surah and what it means to you as a Muslim. I just wanted to highlight one—not even a whole *āyah*—one expression from within one *āyah*; and the expression that this reminder is dedicated to is:

يَٰٓأَيُّهَا ٱلَّذِينَ ءَامَنُواْ ٱجۡتَنِبُواْ كَثِيرٗا مِّنَ ٱلظَّنِّ إِنَّ بَعۡضَ ٱلظَّنِّ إِثۡمٞۖ... ﴿١٢﴾
(الحجرات ٤٩ : ١٢)

Believers, avoid being excessively suspicious, for some suspicion is a sin…

(Al-Ḥujurāt 49: 12)

This is all I'm going to be thinking about with you in this reminder. Roughly translated the *āyah* says, those of you who claim to believe avoid, circumvent or stay away as much as possible from making assumptions (*al-ẓann*)—*inna baʿḍ al-ẓann ithm*—no doubt after assumption comes sin. This is a rough translation of what the *āyah* says. So now let's explore what it's saying at a bit of a deeper level *in shā' Allāh*.

First and foremost I want to tell you that the *āyah* right before it talks about us not making fun of other people—*la yaskhar qawmun min qawm*—it's not okay for you and me to make fun of people, for one group to make fun of another group. If you notice, for instance, the popular comedy industry—stand-up comedians, cartoons that are comical in nature or comedy shows—they'll try to make fun of a particular ethnicity, they'll stereotype something that's funny about the Arab, or they'll stereotype something that's funny about the Mexican, or the black guy, or the white guy, or the Asian guy, or the Indian guy. They'll mock the way they speak or they'll mock the way they dress or the way they eat and everybody gets a laugh out of it. Well this is the *āyah* that says that brand of comedy is no good—*la yaskhar qawmun min qawm*—you shouldn't do this.

It is not something that breeds respect for other people in a culture. It actually breeds this idea of intolerance and looking at other people as something to laugh at or something beneath you, and seeing yourself as superior. However that's not my topic here; the topic is the one about assumptions but I am telling you that assumptions come as a result of that kind of comedy. Once it starts: 'I'm just making a joke... I'm just saying... I'm just kidding'; and you do enough of that, it starts sinking into your head that those people are actually like that. So it starts off as jokes but eventually it just becomes a conviction. You are convinced that those people, that you've been making fun of for so long, are exactly the way the jokes say they are. And by the way, this is not just about ethnicities it is also about religions, it's also about people of different faiths, for example Indo-Paks love making fun of Hindus and Sikhs. That is unacceptable. It's national too, Bangladeshis can have Pakistani jokes and Pakistanis can have Bangladeshi jokes, and it's funny, it's funny to them. But you know what? You think it's just a joke but eventually it becomes a stereotype, a kind of bigotry that's accepted in a society.

It just becomes acceptable to them and they end up violating every time they make a joke like that, they reinforce that stereotype. So when they look at a person from a different ethnicity and even the thought crosses their mind—a judgement passes in their head—even that becomes an evil thing to do. This is what is remarkable about this *āyah*: you don't normally find in the Qur'an us being reprimanded for thinking. You may have learned before that actions we will be answerable for; if you thought about something—some bad thought that came into your head but you didn't act on it—it was just a thought that came in your head, then you're still okay!

But you know what? There are a few exceptions to that, for example, intentions are a thought and even though your action may be good if your intention is corrupt, that thought can dictate how that action counts. Another remarkable and unique exception to that is this *āyah—ijtanibū kathīran min al-ẓann*—Allah says stay, as much as possible, away from this concept of *ẓann*, which I am translating as 'making assumptions'. But the idea of making assumptions is just something that is going on in your head, you didn't say anything, you didn't do anything and even that Allah is saying: don't even think like that. That's a very strange thing about this *āyah*, in that the previous *āyah* said don't make fun of people, that's understandable, that's actually saying something, doing something, it's an action. Later on in this *āyah*, it says: don't spy on people, don't backbite people, right? All of these are actions that people do. They spy against one another, they try to dig up dirt against one another—'don't do that stuff'—fine; but here we're being taught to change the way we think and this is critical.

We're learning something very powerful about this process. If you don't change the way people think, if you don't change the way you and I think, then things are not going to get better; things are going to get worse. Actually the crimes that Allah mentions after that: *ghībah* (backbiting) that you've heard many times about, spying on one another, not trusting each other; all of that actually begins with a certain kind of thinking. And Allah says stay, as much as possible, away from that kind of thinking. So let's begin looking into that a little now, *in shā' Allāh*.

Let's take the word *ijtināb* first. *Ijtināb* originally comes from the word *janb* in Arabic which means the 'side' of something. So when people lie down on their sides—*wa-ʿalā junūbihim* (*Āl ʿImrān* 3: 191)—they are lying on their sides. When you are travelling on a plane, or you're sitting on a subway, or you're sitting on a bus and there is a 'person next to you', this is: *al-ṣāḥib bi-l-janb* (*al-Nisā'* 4: 36). When you're sitting in a waiting room in a hotel, or a hospital, or a doctor's office, and there is a 'person sitting next to you', this is *al-ṣāḥib bi-l-janb*, because they are sitting right by your 'side'.

Now from it comes an interesting verb *al-ijtināb* which means 'to avoid something that is right next to you'. It literally means 'avoidance' but how does it mean avoidance? It's not just to avoid something that's far away, but it's rather something that's actually right next to you. You are in danger of being contaminated by it, so you have to go out of your way to get away from it. What we're learning then is the idea that making assumptions about people is inevitable. It's always there, it's always right next to you it's not something you say, 'Well, I don't judge people man, I don't judge people. I'm not like that'. Actually it's always there. The *iftiʿāl* (*ijtināb*) form in the Arabic language suggests you have to make an effort to do something, it doesn't come naturally. It's not something you do without even thinking about it. It takes effort.

So it doesn't matter that you haven't done it before, you still have to make an effort not to do it now. It's not something that becomes passive, it's not like breathing. So *ijtanibū* means whatever Allah is telling us to stay away from, we must have an active mind, we have to be vigilant and realize that we are always going to be in danger of making that mistake. Nobody can assume that they're righteous and pure enough that they won't fall into this mistake. Had this not been a danger Allah (*ʿazza wa-jall*) could very easily have told us: *lā taẓunnū*. That's a simple command (*amr*). *Khayr al-kalām mā qall wa-dall*: the best kind of speech is concise. 'Don't make assumptions'—*lā taẓunnū*. Don't make assumptions about each other. The language is concise. But He says: *ijtanibū kathīran min al-ẓann*. This is actually *iṭālah* (long-windedness) in rhetoric. You've extended the speech, you've said a lot more than just, 'don't make assumptions'. Rather: 'stay away from it because it's always going to be right next to you'.

Then He adds the word *kathīran* (a lot/very much), which is also strange. When *Ibrahim* (*ʿalayhi al-salām*) makes *duʿā'*: *wa-jnubnī wa-baniyya an naʿbud al-aṣnām* (*Ibrāhīm* 14: 35), he doesn't add the word *kathīran* (a lot)—'Prevent me and my children from worshipping idols'.

When Allah says: *wa-jtanib al-ṭāghūt* (*al-Naḥl* 16: 36), 'avoid false gods', He doesn't say *kathīran* (a lot). He also says: *wa-jtanib al-ṭāghūt* and not *wa-jtanib min al-ṭāghūt*; whereas in the *āyah* we're looking at, He says *min al-ẓann*. That's going even further, meaning making assumptions is so close to you, you have to push it away from you and you have do it a lot. In other words virtually every conversation you and I have has the possibility of our making assumptions about someone. We've got to think about this a lot, we've got to become very conscious of this, if we're going to live by this. Before I discuss how we should avoid it, let's deal with the word *ẓann* a little bit.

What does *ẓann* mean and where does it come from in the Arabic language? It's from what's called *lughat al-aḍdād*: it's from the language of opposites. In other words it means to make assumptions about something, obviously when you make assumptions about something you don't know for sure. You don't really know what you are talking about. But *ẓann* also means that your assumption grows to the point where now you are absolutely convinced of something. It actually means both of those things. That is why in the positive sense you find it in the Qur'an:

ٱلَّذِينَ يَظُنُّونَ أَنَّهُم مُّلَـٰقُوا۟ رَبِّهِمْ ... ﴿٤٦﴾

(البقرة ٢ : ٤٦)

> who realize that ultimately they will have to meet their Lord ...
>
> (Al-Baqarah 2: 46)

They are absolutely convinced that they are going to be meeting with their master—that's a kind of conviction. Before *īmān* they had an assumption: 'Am I going to meet Allah or not, I don't know?' There's just a thought. After *īmān* it became firm *ẓann*, it became conviction—*alladhīna yaẓunnūn annahum mulāqū*

Rabbihim. On the other hand there are people who say things like, 'We are not going to be raised after we die':

... وَمَا يُهْلِكُنَآ إِلَّا ٱلدَّهْرُ ۚ وَمَا لَهُم بِذَٰلِكَ مِنْ عِلْمٍ ۖ إِنْ هُمْ إِلَّا يَظُنُّونَ ﴿٢٤﴾

(الجاثية ٤٥ : ٢٤)

> ... and it is only (the passage of) time that destroys us. Yet the fact is that they know nothing about this and are only conjecturing.
>
> (Al-Jāthiyah 45: 24)

They say: 'We're not going to be raised after we die', and Allah says: 'They have no knowledge about that, they're just making assumptions'. This verb is like an oxymoron.

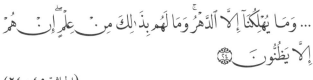

But what does it mean here? Here in particular. It means first you have an assumption about somebody: 'I don't like that guy. I don't know, the guy is kind of…'. Somebody walks into the masjid: 'Man, that guy didn't even have a beard—*astagfiru-Llāh al-ʿaẓīm*!' 'This guy's wearing trousers—dressing like the *kuffār*! What's wrong with this guy?' You look at someone and you size them up. You didn't make any judgements, yet as time progresses you become absolutely convinced and confident that they're all like this. 'All the Africans are like that; all the Senegalese are like that; all the Nigerians are like that; all the Bangladeshis are like that; all the Turks are like that; man I know them all, you don't know those guys. I know.' That's *ẓann*. You're so completely convinced. You're so completely set in your assumptions.

Allah (*ʿazza wa-jall*) says *ijtanibū kathīran min al-ẓann,* it's not even about other ethnicities. Even inside our own homes. The wife says something to you and you assume she means something bad. The husband says something to the wife and she assumes he's trying to make fun of her. 'Dinners really good today', the husband says. 'Oh you hate it again, huh? I know what you really mean.' 'No no, I meant it's good.' 'No, I know what you really mean, I know you.' That's *ẓann*. You're not telepathic; you don't know what the other person means. Learn to give the benefit of the doubt. *Ẓann* can become so bad in some people that two people are walking by each other one of them says, *al-salām ʿalaykum wa-raḥmat Allāh wa-barakātuh*, the other in an angry mumble says, '*Wa-ʿalaykum al-salām*'. 'I know what he meant by "*al-salām ʿalaykum*". He wanted to see if I would say "*Wa-ʿalaykum al-salām*" because he wants to feel like he's better than me'. Or someone might say: 'Why'd he say it like that?' 'What do you mean? He just said *salām*.' 'Yeah, but he said it a certain way…he looked at me a certain way. I know what he was doing.'

There are some of you reading this; I'm not talking about you, I'm really not. But some of you will say to yourselves, 'Is he writing about me?' 'Did somebody tell him about me?' I've given a *khuṭbah* before on a similar topic, it was about speaking nicely: *wa-qūlū li-l-nās husnā* (*al-Baqarah* 2: 83). The entire *khuṭbah* was about speaking nicely because we really need it. We don't need the whole *āyah* just yet. Let's just start with that because we're pretty bad at that, you know. So I gave that *khuṭbah*, and part of it was about not making assumptions, and to just be nice to people when you speak to them. A brother comes up to me afterwards and says, 'Who paid you to give this *khuṭbah*?' 'Did he tell you about me?' My goodness! You know, this is *ẓann*.

You cannot assume that somebody doesn't mean good for you. If someone is proposing something to you or giving you some advice, you cannot assume it's to one up you, to crush your pride or to humiliate you. It may be that they actually mean well for you. If *ẓann* takes over then we are no longer able to give each other good advice any more. I can't come to you as a brother and say, 'Look, I am concerned about this one thing' because you're going to have too much of an assumption against me, and you won't be able to take my advice. You're going to think I have some other agenda.

This *ẓann* isn't just in our interactions within our families or within our community this happens between us and the *duʿāt* and ulama of Islam. Somebody says,

'Man, don't listen to that guy, that one time he said one thing and that means he must be evil, he's got an agenda'. Look, our ulama are not prophets, our *duʿāt* are not prophets, everyone after the *rusul* of Allah (*subḥānahu wa-taʿālā*) will make a mistake in something they say; they're human beings. *Li-kull jawād kabwah wa-li-kull ʿālim hafwah*—every horse has its missteps, and every *ʿālim* makes mistakes. So there is always going to be something that a scholar says that wasn't perfect. Or you won't agree with it, even though you're not a scholar, you decide you don't agree with this one thing that he said. This doesn't take away from all of the good that they did, or they continue to do. You cannot reduce people to one thing that they have said. You can't!

Imagine if people did that to you and me? Imagine if somebody remembered one thing I said, five years ago, and therefore nobody should ever listen to me again. We say things. We're human beings. But to take one thing and to make the assumption about the character of a person and to completely character assassinate them! Then on top of that, there are people who don't even listen to Islamic lectures, read books or listen to *durūs* because they want to benefit, they sit in them waiting for something they can find to attack. 'I'm gonna write this, did he say that? Oh! did he say that? Wow!' They came with *ẓann*, they came and sat in this thing that they are supposed to get closer to Allah with, but the only intention was *ẓann*. 'I'm going to take this part out, I'm going to make a video out of that, then I'm going to write a refutation about this and then I'm gonna…'

Oh my God! What is wrong with you? Don't you have anything better to do? Why so much *ẓann*? Why seeking out what somebody else said wrong? We are so busy finding mistakes in each other we have no time left to share something good with each other. Is the entire ummah already familiar with the Book of Allah that we have time to talk about what you said wrong and what I said wrong or what somebody else said wrong? We don't have time for this, we're not worth the energy; we're not worth the effort. The word of Allah needs to be spread and we're too busy just confirming our *ẓunūn*, that's what we are busy with.

This is what Allah says: *ijtanibū kathīran min al-ẓann*. But that's not the entirety of my reminder. This is the last part of it: *inna baʿd al-ẓann ithm*—no doubt about it, some assumptions are sinful. He says: 'No doubt about it'—it's ironic that Allah put that there. On the one hand, assumptions were things that originally you had doubt over and eventually you became convinced of. But He says let me tell you something in which there is no doubt. *Al-Ithm bi-maʿnā al-jazāʾ kadhālik*—*Ithm* can also mean to give recompense or *jazāʾ*. *Ithm* also means compensation. In other words it's not just any sin; it is a sin that you will be seeing the price for. You will pay the price for it and others will see the consequences of it. It's not just some sin that the angels wrote down and you never saw what happened, only on judgement day will you see. No, you will see the evils of it in this *dunyā* too.

You will see the evils of making assumptions in this *dunyā*. The brotherhood will be destroyed; families will be ripped apart because of people just assuming what the other meant. Nations, entire nations will be willing to go to war because of an assumption. How many political scandals happen because of assumptions? There's a rumour spread that this politician did this, there is no evidence yet but riots have already started in the streets. People have already started to die and businesses have already started to be ruined. It doesn't matter which country it is, the fact is that based on a rumour, based on a *ẓann* some people died!

How serious is this thing? It's not just something that ruins your personal life or a community's life. It can ruin entire countries. It can ruin entire nations. Can you imagine, for example, the wars that we went to based on assumptions? We sold the assumption that there are weapons of mass destruction, didn't we? Now the reality is known; it's not a hidden thing. How many millions of lives have to be lost because people buy into assumption. *Ijtanibū kathīran min al-ẓann*—this isn't just advice to Muslims, it's advice to all of humanity.

This is why in the next *āyah* Allah (*ʿazza wa-jall*) does not say: *yā ayyuha alladhīna āmanū*—O you who believe; He says: *yā ayyuha al-nās*—O *people*, We made you nations and tribes, We made you into different kinds of ethnicities, different languages, different cultures—*li-taʿārafū*—so you can get to know one another, not so you make fun of each other, not so you make assumptions about each other. That wasn't the point in making you different ethnicities. You didn't realize why I made you like this. Why are we different? You didn't get the point. That address is to all of humanity; but before He addressed all of humanity He said: *yā ayyuha alladhīna āmanū ijtanibū kathīran min al-ẓann*. Why did He say that? What are some of the *ḥikam* in that?

I conclude with this: before addressing all of humanity, He addressed the believers because the Muslims were supposed to be the example of: how you don't stereotype; how you don't make fun of other people; how you don't make assumptions; how you have clean communication; how you give the benefit of the doubt; how you don't pass judgement until you have absolute clarity. Until you have clarity, you don't say anything. You reserve your judgement.

Somebody asks your opinion, 'What do you think about this imam?' 'What do you think about this person?' You say, 'Well, I don't know enough to say, but I think he's pretty bad'. No, no, no! 'I don't know enough to say.' Full stop! It's done! I've got nothing else to say. I'm going to assume he's a good person, I'm almost sure he's a good person. If anything, *jid li-akhīka ʿudhran*: find excuses for your brother.

If you don't know enough just say, 'Look, I don't know, I've only heard things' which obviously is *qīl wa-qāl*—when you hear something bad and you spread it, this is against the teachings of the Prophet (*ṣallā Allāh ʿalayhi wa-sallam*). So when you say, 'You know what I heard...' and you continue your sentence, you just violated something the Prophet (*ṣallā Allāh ʿalayhi wa-sallam*) said. When you start saying, 'You know what I've heard....' 'No never mind, I didn't hear anything. It was somebody else.' Change the subject. Don't finish the sentence, because that's part of spreading *ẓann*. And then the heard, the heard, and the heard goes so far that people just start making all kinds of assumptions, then start making decisions based on those assumptions—*subḥān Allāh*.

We have to become people that see clarity. Until something is *absolutely clear*, we don't take a step forward, we never take a step forward. This is in family life, this is in work life, this is in community life, this is even in terms of the news sometimes we hear things in the news that are outrageous and we assume that it's true. An entire machine built on the idea of selling fear, how can we trust it? There has to be more thorough investigative journalism before we make assumptions about an entire people or events. We have to develop a scepticism when: *in jā'akum fāsiq bi-naba' fa-tabayyanū* (*al-Ḥujurāt* 49: 6)—when a corrupt source comes to you with news then clarify it. Don't just listen to it *fa-tabayyanū*, and in another *qirā'ah* (variant reading), *fa-tathabbatū*. Until you are absolutely firm about what it actually is, do not pass judgement. Do not make assumptions.

May Allah (*'azza wa-jall*) help us live according to these principles that can make our lives, the lives of our families and the life of our community and the ummah so much better than it is today. May Allah (*'azza wa-jall*) help us to become those who don't look for flaws in what other people are saying but rather develop sincerity towards others, a love towards others. And may Allah (*'azza wa-jall*) use the message of this *dīn* not to spread differences among us but to unite us as a people and bring our hearts closer together.

CHAPTER 5

Leadership

Often times, it's easy to talk about how great the Prophet (*ṣallā Allāh ʿalayhi wa-sallam*) was, and what an incredible example he was, but it's very difficult to put a mirror to ourselves and discover how far we are from the example he left. Allah (*ʿazza wa-jall*) did not make him an incredible example just for us to praise the example; He made him that example so we can live up, as best we can, to that example. In this particular *āyah* Allah (*ʿazza wa-jall*) highlights a quality of leadership. The *Rasūl* of Allah (*ṣallā Allāh ʿalayhi wa-sallam*) played many roles: the role of a father, a husband, a friend, a neighbour, he played many roles but in this particular *āyah* Allah (*ʿazza wa-jall*) highlights his role as a leader. And before I go into it, I want us, myself included, to remember that when we learn something about the Messenger of Allah (*ṣallā Allāh ʿalayhi wa-sallam*) we have to think: how does that affect me as a leader? Many of you sitting reading this are going to be saying, 'Well, I'm not a leader, so this doesn't apply to me'. As a matter of fact, for every member of this ummah [Allah says]:

كُنتُمْ خَيْرَ أُمَّةٍ أُخْرِجَتْ لِلنَّاسِ ... ﴿١١٠﴾

(آل عمران ٣: ١١٠)

You are now the best nation brought forth for mankind...

(Āl ʿImrān 3: 110)

In some capacity we have all been given a position of leadership. All of us. Some of our leadership roles are more obvious than others, every man that has a wife, has children; is the leader of their household. You're leading your household, and so when you learn something about the leadership of *Rasūl Allāh* (*ṣallā Allāh ʿalayhi wa-sallam*), and I learn something about it, I have to apply it to my family. Some of you are managers at the office so you have to apply this to your employees because you're leaders over them. Some of you are teachers and you're leaders of your classroom so you have to apply it to that. Some of you are in leadership positions in organizations or at *masājid* or schools, in any of those capacities, you are responsible over people. Whether it's part time or full time, whether it's a little bit or a lot, it doesn't matter but in pretty much every institution that human beings belong to, there's a hierarchy and there's leadership. And in many of those cases you happen to be in a position of leadership. It may not be absolute leadership, it may be limited, but still it is there. Bear in mind that recognition, that it's really not just talking about *Rasūl Allāh* (*ṣallā Allāh ʿalayhi wa-sallam*) but through his legacy, it's talking to all of us and *bi-idhni-Llāh taʿālā*, we can benefit from these beautiful *āyāt* and this one particularly beautiful *āyah*.

Allah (*ʿazza wa-jall*) revealed this *āyah* in the context of the Battle of Uḥud. In *Sūrat Āl ʿImrān* Allah talks extensively—sixty or so *āyāt* are dedicated to the discussion about what went wrong at Uḥud, and this is after the fact. In other words, Allah did not reveal these *āyāt* before the battle but rather these *āyāt* came down after the battle. Many of you are familiar, some of you need a reminder; the Battle of Badr was an incredible success. In the Battle of Badr the Muslims were able to fight against a massive army, a much more prepared much more outnumbering army of Quraish and still annihilate seventy of their leaders. But the Battle of Uḥud was the exact opposite.

It started out just like Badr; we were winning in the beginning and then, because of one strategic mistake made by the archers who the *Rasūl* of Allah (*ṣallā Allāh ʿalayhi wa-sallam*) appointed on the mountain. You could call them snipers today but they were archers back then. He appointed them to stay in their place and he told them even if you see birds eating from our corpses, in other words, every one of us is dead, don't you move from there. Don't move from there. They, however, saw the opposite, they didn't see the Muslims dying and birds eating off of their corpses, they saw that the Muslims were actually destroying the enemy.

وَلَقَدْ صَدَقَكُمُ ٱللَّهُ وَعْدَهُۥٓ إِذْ تَحُسُّونَهُم بِإِذْنِهِۦ ... ﴿١٥٢﴾
(آل عمران ٣: ١٥٢)

> Allah surely fulfilled His promise (of succour) when you were slaying them by His leave ...
>
> (Āl ʿImrān 3: 152)

Allah Himself says: Allah fulfilled His promise to you when you were making the enemy feel the heat of battle, you were annihilating the enemy; you were driving them away.

The enemy was making a run for it in the Battle of Uḥud, that's Allah's own description. That's the time where there was a disagreement among the archers and some of them decided. No, no, no, the Prophet (*ṣallā Allāh ʿalayhi wa-sallam*) said don't come down, even if you see us dying but this is the opposite case, we're actually winning, so it's okay, that's not what he meant.

So there was a disagreement among them and by the way, that's a separate topic, how do you deal with disagreements? That's not my topic here. Actually if you look at it, the disagreement among those *Ṣaḥābah* was a legitimate difference of opinion. It was not that some decided to disobey the Messenger and the others did not, that's not the case. They actually both looked at the same statement of the Prophet (*ṣallā Allāh ʿalayhi wa-sallam*) and interpreted it in two different ways. This happens on multiple occasions among the *Ṣaḥābah*, the problem wasn't that they interpreted it differently; the problem was they broke the chain of command. The *Ṣaḥābī* left in charge, the battalion commander—his decision was 'we stay'. And when the Prophet (*ṣallā Allāh ʿalayhi wa-sallam*) leaves somebody in charge, you have to listen to him even if you have a difference of opinion. That was the real problem. But that's a separate topic.

In any case they come down, Khālid ibn al-Walīd who we say now (*raḍiya Allāh ʿanhu*) at that time he wasn't Muslim yet. He was an experienced military man, so he sees from the corner of his eye that the Muslims have left their strategic, sniper post. He rendezvouses, he comes around and flanks the Muslims from behind and the entire scene of battle turns upside down. It's chaos, all hell breaks loose. The Muslims don't know where the enemy is coming from, what's going on; even the Messenger (*ṣallā Allāh ʿalayhi wa-sallam*) was hit so hard he fell unconscious. His tooth fell out and he fell unconscious and when he woke up his face was filled with blood. While he was passed out a rumour spread that the Prophet (*ṣallā Allāh ʿalayhi wa-sallam*) had been killed. Allah (*ʿazza wa-jall*) revealed the *āyah*:

وَمَا كَانَ لِنَفْسٍ أَن تَمُوتَ إِلَّا بِإِذْنِ ٱللَّهِ ... ﴿١٤٥﴾
(آل عمران ٣ : ١٤٥)

It is not given to any soul to die except with the leave of Allah ...

(Āl ʿImrān 3: 145)

Wa-mā kāna li-nafs an tamūt illā bi-idhn Allāh: it's not appropriate for a prophet to die—no prophet gets to die—until Allah gives permission. Except that Allah gives permission.

Anyway, this happens and there's so much chaos on the battlefield that people like Umar (*raḍiya Allāh ʿanhu*), you can imagine how big an asset Umar (*raḍiya Allāh ʿanhu*) is in the battlefield; he drops his sword and sits on the ground. He goes what's the point now? He got killed, what's the point now? Muslims were demoralized then it was retrieved that the Prophet (*ṣallā Allāh ʿalayhi wa-sallam*) actually is still alive. The Muslims then went into a retreat position and they headed up towards the mountain.

۞ إِذْ تُصْعِدُونَ وَلَا تَلْوُۥنَ عَلَىٰٓ أَحَدٍ ... ﴿١٥٣﴾
(آل عمران ٣ : ١٥٣)

Recall when you were fleeing without casting even a side glance at anyone ...

(Āl ʿImrān 3: 153)

Allah describes when you were running up the mountain, you were scaling the mountain and you wouldn't turn back to look at anyone. In other words you were desperate to save the Messenger (*ṣallā Allāh ʿalayhi wa-sallam*) from this chaotic situation and by the way some people were running ahead and they left the Prophet behind.

... وَٱلرَّسُولُ يَدۡعُوكُمۡ فِيٓ أُخۡرَىٰكُمۡ ... ﴿١٥٣﴾

(آل عمران ٣: ١٥٣)

... and the Messenger was calling out to you from the rear...

(Āl ʿImrān 3: 153)

And the Messenger's calling you from behind you. Then Allah (*ʿazza wa-jall*) gave them the courage to fight back, they turned a little bit of it around but still by the time it was over, seventy of the greatest *Ṣaḥābah* of the ummah were *shahīd*; they had been killed. Including the beloved uncle of the Prophet (*ṣallā Allāh ʿalayhi wa-sallam*), who many of you know the story, when Hind got a hold of him she actually ripped his heart out and chewed on it. And so for the Prophet (*ṣallā Allāh ʿalayhi wa-sallam*) to see his uncle in that state after him almost being killed himself, is a traumatic experience and all of these problems began with what? With one act of disobedience, one act of disobedience and seventy

Ṣaḥābah are killed including the family of the Prophet (*ṣallā Allāh ʿalayhi wa-sallam*).

I want you to think about this, the real test of leadership is not when your followers are following you; the real test of leadership is when your followers disappoint you. When you have all the reasons in the world to be angry at them because they have done something terrible: they did not obey a very simple instruction. They have made a mistake and you can imagine now, after it's all said and done, those archers, those *Ṣaḥābah* who were positioned in those sniper positions, when they're going to be having a meeting with *Rasūl Allāh* (*ṣallā Allāh ʿalayhi wa-sallam*) they are expecting terrible things. They have disappointed their Beloved (*ṣallā Allāh ʿalayhi wa-sallam*); I mean they must be scared for their life.

Let's just put this in perspective a little bit. You mess up at your job, you had a project due, the client was waiting for it but you didn't submit the project. You sent the email but it didn't go through; you thought that it went through. Now you're in big trouble because the client is asking to cancel the contract and your company is going to lose a million dollars and it's your fault. The whole weekend's gone by and on Monday there's going to be a meeting with your boss. What are you expecting in the meeting huh? and that's just about money, this is about lives, this is about family loss, this is about blood. Can you imagine what that meeting has to be like? *Subḥān Allāh*!

And so this meeting is about to happen, Allah reveals an *āyah* to the Prophet (*ṣallā Allāh ʿalayhi wa-sallam*) before he goes to meet with the *Ṣaḥābah*. This is Allah preparing him for this meeting; that's the *āyah*. How does a leader deal with people that have terribly, terribly disappointed him. The *āyah* begins:

فَبِمَا رَحْمَةٍ مِّنَ ٱللَّهِ لِنتَ لَهُمْ ۖ... ﴿١٥٩﴾

(آل عمران ٣: ١٥٩)

(O Prophet), it was thanks to Allah's mercy that you were gentle to them ...

(Āl ʿImrān 3: 159)

It is by the unimaginable, indescribable, mysterious loving mercy of Allah that you are lenient towards them. The language here deserves a lot of attention. Actually, *linta lahum bi-raḥmat Allāh* is the normal Arabic sentence structure for this sentence but when you change the order to: *fa-bi-mā raḥmatin min Allāh* that actually means that this is an unusual kind of *raḥmah* and it is only because of this special gift from Allah of *raḥmah*, of loving mercy that has come from Him to you, that you are going to be able to be nice to them and lenient towards them in the meeting.

The second benefit that I want to highlight here is the word *mā* in the verse *fa-bi-mā raḥmatin min Allāh*.

The grammarians say that the *mā* is extra; you can say *fa-bi-raḥmatin min Allāh*. So the addition of the *mā* actually adds a kind of *taʿajjub* (amazement), they say in *balāghah* (the study of rhetoric). In simple English, it is a shocking level of mercy; it is a shocking level of love and compassion that has come from Allah. Then there is the fact that *raḥmah* is also not *bi-raḥmati Allāh*. In other places in the Qur'an Allah says,

قُلْ بِفَضْلِ ٱللَّهِ وَبِرَحْمَتِهِۦ ... ﴿٥٨﴾

(يونس ١٠ : ٥٨)

Tell them, (O Prophet): "Let them rejoice in Allah's Grace and Mercy ... "

(Yūnus 10: 58)

There is an *iḍafah* (possessive grammatical construct) in *faḍl Allah*—they're connected together. But here He says: *fa-bi-mā raḥmatin min Allāh*. The two are separated with a *min* and the benefit of separating these two is that it creates a mystery: what kind of love and mercy is this? Where did it come from? And then it answers the question: *min Allāh*. There are three or four or five devices just in *fa-bi-mā raḥmatin min Allāh* that are almost impossible to capture in the English translation but the point of them is: the way that Allah has granted the gift of *raḥmah*, of leniency, of softness, of love to the Messenger of Allah and the gift that He gave to the *Ṣaḥābah* also, is beyond description. Because no leader could ever leave an example like this one.

In the military, when soldiers make a mistake; lives are lost. The hearing afterwards is called a court martial. When that hearing is done, typically those soldiers are either executed or sent in prison. That's what happens to them because of insubordination, because they disobeyed a direct order. That's what happens in a usual military scenario. And by the way, this is directly a military scenario, the *Rasūl* (*ṣallā Allāh ʿalayhi wa-sallam*) in this case is not just the leader, he is the General of the Army, and these soldiers are presenting their case. And Allah says, you are exceptional, there is no one like you. Even in this case, you are unusually lenient. It's something that has come from Allah for you.

Then He says *linta*—the words in this *āyah* fascinate me. *linta lahum* which I keep translating as, 'you are lenient towards them'. The word *lāna* in Arabic is the opposite of *khushūnah*: 'ruggedness and harshness'. And harshness could be in your look, harshness could be in your speech, harshness could be in your actions, harshness could be in your gestures, and harshness can also be in your silence. Sometimes you're mad at your son or your daughter and your harshness is not that you yelled at them but your harshness is that you're not talking to them—that you're not making eye contact. Sometimes the mother is upset with the child and the mother doesn't look at the baby but the baby knows, the child knows—Mama's angry. She doesn't have to say anything but there's a kind of *khushūnah*, a ruggedness, a roughness there because of her attitude, her facial expression. When Allah (*ʿazza wa-jall*) told the Messenger (*ṣallā Allāh ʿalayhi wa-sallam*) *linta lahum*, did He specify: how are you lenient towards them? Rather, he left it completely open. In other words, in your speech, in your facial expressions, in your emotions, in your interaction with them, the way you will look towards them, all of it will have to be soft—that is the message from Allah. Before you go into this meeting, let me prepare you—*subḥān Allāh*!

فَبِمَا رَحْمَةٍ مِّنَ ٱللَّهِ لِنتَ لَهُمْ ... ﴿١٥٩﴾

(آل عمران ٣: ١٥٩)

(O Prophet), it was thanks to Allah's mercy that you were gentle to them …

(Āl ʿImrān 3: 159)

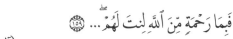

A little bit more about the word *līn* and where this word comes from. They say in Arabic: *talayyana*, when you give somebody compliments to make them feel good, when you describe someone with the best qualities that they have, they describe this as *talayyana*. One of the implications of *linta lahum* is: when you go in there, highlight the good in these people. The meeting is not supposed to be about what is good about them. The meeting is supposed to be what they messed up with—what is bad about them—but when you go, say good things about them. They're depressed enough as it is, they're embarrassed enough as it is about what happened, they're human beings they made a mistake, they came to believe in you and they've made sacrifices for you (*ṣallā Allāh ʿalayhi wa-sallam*) before. And yes, they made a mistake, but it doesn't wipe away all of the good that they have. They need a little bit of a morale boost and something they were not expecting from you. So you need to go in there and say something nice to each of them. *Linta lahum*: you're going to start this meeting by giving a compliment.

This is incredible leadership. Executives pay millions of dollars, companies spend all this money on executive and corporate leadership and boosting morale. Some of you go to those boring meetings, you look at eight hundred power point presentation slides, you fall asleep and at the end of it, 'Yeah, we're going to beat the last year's sales record. YES!' Everybody's in it only for the money; that's all artificial. At the end of the day all of it is artificial. That's not real leadership. Real leadership, the Prophetic model of leadership, the model of Muhammad *Rasūl Allāh* (*ṣallā Allāh ʿalayhi wa-sallam*) is really that people are in servitude, they have become enslaved to those who are good to them. And when you were least expecting that you would be good to your followers, that's when you were good to them—*linta lahum*.

Going further, the word *layn*—I'm still not done with this word because this word really baffles me. The Arabic *ṣāghahā bi-layānihi* means: 'He listened to (the woman), softening his stance'. In other words *'layān'* is used when you listen to someone without passing judgement; you listen to someone after putting your anger aside. I'll give you an example so it's easy to understand: if my daughter got an 'F' in math and I say, 'What happened here? Explain yourself'. I don't care what she says, I'll still be angry. Let's be honest, it's not like she is going to give me a very logical explanation, 'Oh okay, *mā shā' Allāh*. Give me a hug'. It's not going to be like that. I've already made up my mind that I am upset, that decision has already been made. Now it really doesn't matter what she says.

But the expression they use in Arabic, *ṣāghahā bi-layānihi*, means actually he listened to her with full attention, he didn't make up his mind that he is going to be angry anyway. 'Look you made a mistake. The bottom line is: I don't care how you slice it, you messed up.' But no. You're going to listen to them softly too. Not only will you give them softness but when they're speaking you're not going to be angry. You're going to listen calmly and you are going to maintain a soft sense towards them. The word *līn* actually in Arabic also means a soft date that's particularly tasty. You should be like that date, you should be a treat to them—*subḥān Allāh*.

Then the word means *rakhā'*, softness; it means something that gives you comfort, *na'īm*. You should go in there and be a source of comfort for these people; not a source of misery, not a source of sadness, not a source of depression; you should be the other way around. This is about the *Rasūl* of Allah (*ṣallā Allāh 'alayhi wa-sallam*) so far, but you know what? This is also about us, we're leaders too aren't we? When the wife disappoints you, when the child disappoints you, when the employee disappoints you, when the friend disappoints you, what's our reaction? How do we respond? How do we deal with it? And by the way, the *Rasūl* of Allah (*ṣallā Allāh 'alayhi wa-sallam*) is being told to calm down and be the nicest he can be in a situation where loved ones have been killed! But we lose our temper over keys that are lost, over a cell phone you can't find, over a phone call that she didn't pick up. Over that? Can you imagine? How far removed? And then we say we love the *Sunnah* of the Prophet (*ṣallā Allāh 'alayhi wa-sallam*). What position are we in to talk like that? This is the legacy he (*ṣallā Allāh 'alayhi wa-sallam*) left, this is the leadership Allah is teaching him.

Thank Allah we are not put in that position; we are not put in that position, because that is a real leader who can handle that kind of a situation.

The *āyāt* go on with remarkable words:

...وَلَوْ كُنتَ فَظًّا غَلِيظَ ٱلْقَلْبِ لَٱنفَضُّوا۟ مِنْ حَوْلِكَ ... ﴿١٥٩﴾
(آل عمران ٣: ١٥٩)

> ... Had you been rough, hardhearted, they would surely have scattered away from you ...
>
> (Āl ʿImrān 3: 159)

Faẓẓ actually means a few things in Arabic, and I'll highlight each of them. First it means *kashin al-kalām*: someone who speaks in a harsh, mean, nasty way. *Faẓẓ* literally has to do with speaking to somebody and *afẓaẓtuhū* actually means I sprayed him or I poured dust on someone. In other words, when somebody's yelling at the top of their lungs and there's almost spit coming out of their mouth—this is *faẓẓ*. If you were screaming at the top of your lungs and you were yelling and scolding them, if you walked into that meeting and said, 'WHAT HAPPENED? What did you people do?' If you did that; this is what Allah is saying: 'had you been that way...'—*wa-law kunta faẓẓan*.

And sometimes there are people who say, 'Well I say mean things but I still love you inside. I mean, I yell at you, and I yell at you at the top of my lungs, but give me a hug afterwards'. Some parents do that, some parents lose their cool, they go crazy, they go Hulk on their kids and then afterwards they're like, 'I still love you, it's okay. You want to get some ice cream?' You know what? It doesn't undo it. The damage is done. Allah (*'azza wa-jall*) before He says: 'You shouldn't be hard in your heart', He first says: 'You need to watch your tongue'. *Wa-law kunta faẓẓan*—first—*ghalīẓ al-qalb*—second. *Ghalīẓ al-qalb* means 'hard of the heart'. In other words, inside you developed a grudge against them, you can't have that either.

So there are two problems: one, speaking in an angry way even if it's 'I love you, but you messed up!' No, no, no, you can't do that either. First of all, you've got to speak very softly; and second, sometimes people speak softly but they are holding a grudge inside. The mother is saying, the father is saying, the husband is saying, 'I'm not angry' but he is angry, he's got something inside, 'Yeah, I hate when you do this, I'm not going to say anything but, man, I'm burning inside'.

Allah adds the second problem: *ghalīẓ al-qalb*. *Ghilẓah* in Arabic is something impenetrable: *mā lā yadkhul fīhi shay'*—something which you cannot penetrate. If your heart becomes so hard, you are so disappointed with these people, that you have written them off. Even if you are speaking nicely to them, you've basically written them off. You've given up on them—they are no good to you. This is *ghilẓat al-qalb*.

So there are two things here about the *Rasūl* (*ṣallā Allāh ʿalayhi wa-sallam*): on the other hand, when you go in there, be nice. Your face shouldn't look depressed, you should make them feel comfortable, say good things about them, calm them down, when they speak listen softly. You need to be able to control all of your emotions, and all of that sadness; put it away when you deal with your followers. And on the other hand, if you didn't do these things and if you were like any other leader, who would lose their cool, what would happen? *La-nfaḍḍū min ḥawlik*—with the *lām* of emphasis. Some ulama say about this *lām* that Allah effectively swears here; Allah swears to the fact that the *Ṣaḥābah* would have run away from you. They would have run away—this is in the Qur'an guys, this is in the Qur'an! The *Ṣaḥābah* would have run away from *Rasūl Allāh* (*ṣallā Allāh ʿalayhi wa-sallam*), Allah swears by it; if he was mean.

If he was mean; the Messenger would still be speaking the truth, he would still be the recipient of the Qur'an, he would still be saying *Lā ilāha illa Allāh*, he would still be teaching, all of the evidences would still be there but one thing would be missing—his softness. And Allah says, even that much is enough for these *Ṣaḥābah*, who are willing to die for you, they are dying for the sake of Allah (*ʿazza wa-jall*), and even they—Allah guarantees it—would have run away from you.

And what is *infiḍāḍ*, when the verse says *la-nfaḍḍū min ḥawlik*. *Infiḍāḍ* in Arabic means when you drop a cup, or a glass and it shatters and all the pieces of glass run away from each other. You know why that's described? Not *la-farrū*—they would have run away from you—or *la-abaqū min ḥawlik*—they would have escaped from you. No, no, no: *la-nfaḍḍū min ḥawlik*. Why *infiḍāḍ*? Because when a glass breaks, you can't put it back together. They will run away from you in a way, they'll never come back; and even if they do, it will never be like the unity that they once had. This is the lesson of leadership taught to *Rasūl Allāh* (*ṣallā Allāh ʿalayhi wa-sallam*): *la-nfaḍḍū min ḥawlik*—you cannot afford to be like this to them.

We are very good at getting angry. Muslims, *mā shā' Allāh*, we're very good at getting angry. Everything makes us angry. You know what really should make us angry? How far we are from the legacy that the Prophet (*ṣallā Allāh ʿalayhi wa-sallam*) left, how far we are from the word of Allah, how bad we are at controlling our temper; that should make us mad at ourselves, not anybody else.

What do you do after that? The *āyah* is not done, and I have to conclude; but you know as this *kalām*, this speech, this orientation—leadership training from Allah to *Rasūl* (*ṣallā Allāh ʿalayhi wa-sallam*) concludes—what does He tell him? He tells him:

... فَٱعْفُ عَنْهُمْ وَٱسْتَغْفِرْ لَهُمْ وَشَاوِرْهُمْ فِى ٱلْأَمْرِ فَإِذَا عَزَمْتَ
فَتَوَكَّلْ عَلَى ٱللَّهِ إِنَّ ٱللَّهَ يُحِبُّ ٱلْمُتَوَكِّلِينَ ﴿١٥٩﴾
(آل عمران ٣: ١٥٩)

... So pardon them, and pray for their forgiveness, and take counsel from them in matters of importance. And when you are resolved on a course of action put your trust in Allah. Surely Allah loves those who put their trust (in Him).
(Āl ʿImrān 3: 159)

Then you know what you do? You go and be nice and all of that, but you need to pardon them and move on—*faʿfu ʿanhum*, lovingly pardon them. *Wa-staghfir lahum*, and make *istighfār* for them, ask Allah to forgive them. There's nothing between you and me, we're good. I'm no longer angry; I'm already being nice to you, that's number one. Number two, when the meeting is over and you are going to go make *duʿā'*, you're going to make *duʿā'* for the *maghfirah* of Ḥamzah (*raḍiya Allāh ʿanhu*), you're going to make *duʿā'* for the entrance into *jannah* of all of those *shuhadā'*; you will also make *duʿā'* for the archers who started this mess. You will make *duʿā'* for them. This will be your true test of leadership. You know that you have nothing left in your heart, when you are making *duʿā'* for your parents, when you are making *duʿā'* for your loved ones; you can make *duʿā'* for those who disappointed you, those who messed up: that's a leader.

And by the way, this *duʿā'* is not in public, you don't walk into the meeting and start the meeting by saying, 'May Allah forgive you people!' No, no, no, this is in private. Making *duʿā'* in public is a spectacle, you're just embarrassing people. This is your way of blaming them; but in private when you're begging Allah, in your own time, then you made time to beg for them, the ones who disappointed you, and said to Allah, '*Yā Rabb* these are just followers, they made a mistake *kull banī Ādam khaṭṭā'ūn* (all of the Children of Adam make mistakes). Forgive their mistake, let them move on from this, make them stronger, and don't put hatred for them in the hearts of other Muslims'. This is the *duʿā'* you make for them—*wa-staghfir lahum*.

But it's not over yet. The next time there's a meeting, call the people who disappointed you. Have them join the meeting, and not only have them join the meeting, when an important decision comes up, you ask them, 'What do you think? I'd like to hear your opinion'. And don't just listen to their opinion for an artificial: 'Hey, tell me what you think?' and whatever they say, you respond: '*Jazak Allah khayran*!' No, no, no. Actually consult their opinion: *wa-shāwirhum fī al-'amr*, take their consultation in matters of decision. Take whose consultation? The same people who disappointed you.

Imagine, the same people who disappointed *Rasūl Allāh* (*ṣallā Allāh ʿalayhi wa-sallam*) in the Battle of Uḥud, when there's a meeting happening for the Battle of Aḥzāb, he calls the same *Ṣaḥābah* and says: 'What do you think we should do?' And they're like: 'Who? What? Me!? You want my opinion!? I just messed up last time'. No, no, no, I need your opinion, I value your opinion. And this *Ṣaḥābī* will say this can only be the Messenger of Allah (*ṣallā Allāh ʿalayhi wa-sallam*) because no man has a heart that big. This has to come from Allah. That's why the *āyah* begins: *fa-bi-mā raḥmatin min Allāh*. We don't discard people's opinion because they disappointed us in the past; and we don't just, artificially take their opinion. A lot of times we listen to people but we don't *really* listen to them; we just go through the exercise but it's just artificial. We shouldn't be doing that. Whatever the Messenger (*ṣallā Allāh ʿalayhi wa-sallam*) does; he does with sincerity—*wa-shāwirhum fī al-'amr.*

Then finally when you make a decision: *fa-idhā ʿazamta fa-tawakkal ʿalā Allāh*—then when you reach the final decision, then trust Allah. Because the decision you people reach, and that you (*ṣallā Allāh ʿalayhi wa-sallam*) reach, that is not a guarantee of success. The guarantee of success comes from Allah, so trust Allah after you make a decision. *Inna Allāh yuḥibb al-mutawakkilīn*—no doubt Allah loves those who put their trust in Him.

What are we learning at the end? We don't trust our leadership and our leadership doesn't even trust itself, at the end of the day, all of us trust Allah (*ʿazza wa-jall*). We do the best we can and whatever decisions we make, at the end of it we don't say, 'I'm the leader, I made this decision, and it's the best decision'. No, we say, 'I made this decision, *yā Rabb*. Put *khayr* in it because this decision doesn't just affect me, it affects all of my followers. It affects the whole family, it affects everything; so *yā Allāh* put *khayr* in this decision. I don't know if it's the best. They have relied upon me because they rely upon You'. This is a beautiful, beautiful sampling of the *Rasūl*'s legacy of leadership (*ṣallā Allāh ʿalayhi wa-sallam*) and I pray that we're able to get even an ounce of this into our personal lives, even a little bit of it into our family lives, into our business lives, into our professional lives, into our community life then *wa-Llāhi* the *barakāt* of the *Sunnah*; the blessings of the *Sunnah*, when we really apply leadership, is that people love each other for the sake of Allah. And when you don't apply leadership principles, people start hating each other, people start getting angry at each other. This kills anger. This puts out the fire.

May Allah (*ʿazza wa-jall*) make us of the people who are able to have soft hearts towards their fellow Muslims and recognize the value and appreciation of forgiving one another and moving forward.

PART III

OUR FINANCIAL DEALINGS

CHAPTER 6

How We Earn

In this reminder, I wanted to reflect with you on a few *āyāt* belonging to the fourth surah of the Qur'an, *Sūrat al-Nisā'*. Those of you who aren't familiar with *Sūrat al-Nisā'*, it is one of the earlier revelations in Madinah after the Prophet (*ṣallā Allāh ʿalayhi wa-sallam*) migrated to the city. Now just a little bit of background so everything is put into perspective. When the Prophet (*ṣallā Allāh ʿalayhi wa-sallam*) moves to Madinah, there are the beginnings of a Muslim community. Back in Makkah, you could think of them as a non-violent resistance movement, but that's all they were, they weren't a community yet. They weren't even allowed, in most instances, to pray in public. They were a persecuted small bunch and they were seen as a fringe element in Makkah. But once the migration happens and there is a community already ripe for the message of Islam—a couple of tribes have already accepted Islam and they are welcoming the Prophet (*ṣallā Allāh*

ʿalayhi wa-sallam), almost as a mayor into that city, and he takes this position of authority.

There were, of course, Jewish and Christian communities in Madinah at the time, and a treaty is formed between the Muslim, Jewish and Christian communities for a joint collaboration to defend the city together and so on. These are the preliminary workings of the Prophet (*ṣallā Allāh ʿalayhi wa-sallam*) in the first six months that he got there. More and more of the Qur'an is getting revealed and now the Qur'an includes instructions or laws. You'll notice most of the Makkan Qur'an doesn't have a lot of laws and that is two thirds of the Qur'an. Here and there, there are some ethical instructions but for the most part there isn't what we call Shariah, technically. Of course a few elements of the Shariah were already there like prayer, but when the Prophet (*ṣallā Allāh ʿalayhi wa-sallam*) comes to Madinah more and more of the Shariah is coming down.

This surah is particularly important because this was a Muslim community in its infancy—it's just starting—this is what is going to eventually be a fifth of the world's population. A civilization that spans continents and ethnicities. But right now it's in its infancy—just a few hundred people at the most, and so Allah is going to reveal to them instructions that will make sure that they are founded on the right foundation. When you build a tall building, you have to have a deep foundation; and the deeper your foundation the taller you can build. If you don't take the time to build your foundation then you can't go very high. Now that is also true of our faith in terms of our theology; our beliefs are supposed to be rooted in a lot of depth. We're supposed to really understand what it is that we believe and find conviction in it, so that our actions can reflect that. That's on the one hand. But even within the Shariah, even within the laws themselves, Allah revealed introductory laws that set the stage for the refining of the later laws, and this is part of what I wanted to share with you. At the very base of an infant Muslim community, what is one of the most important instructions?

Allah (*ʿazza wa-jall*) says:

يَٰٓأَيُّهَا ٱلَّذِينَ ءَامَنُواْ لَا تَأۡكُلُوٓاْ أَمۡوَٰلَكُم بَيۡنَكُم بِٱلۡبَٰطِلِ إِلَّآ أَن تَكُونَ تِجَٰرَةً عَن تَرَاضٖ مِّنكُمۡۚ وَلَا تَقۡتُلُوٓاْ أَنفُسَكُمۡۚ إِنَّ ٱللَّهَ كَانَ بِكُمۡ رَحِيمٗا ٢٩

(النساء ٤ : ٢٩)

Believers! Do not devour one another's possessions wrongfully; rather, let there be trading by mutual consent; and do not kill yourselves. Surely Allah is ever Compassionate to you.

(Al-Nisāʾ 4: 29)

Those of you who claim to believe don't consume each other's monies using falsehood. Do not engage in shady financial transactions. This has occurred already in *Sūrat al-Baqarah*, Allah (*'azza wa-jall*) there says:

وَلَا تَأْكُلُوٓا۟ أَمْوَٰلَكُم بَيْنَكُم بِٱلْبَٰطِلِ وَتُدْلُوا۟ بِهَآ إِلَى ٱلْحُكَّامِ
لِتَأْكُلُوا۟ فَرِيقًا مِّنْ أَمْوَٰلِ ٱلنَّاسِ بِٱلْإِثْمِ وَأَنتُمْ تَعْلَمُونَ ﴿١٨٨﴾
(البقرة ٢ : ١٨٨)

> Do not usurp one another's possessions by false means, nor proffer your possessions to the authorities so that you may sinfully and knowingly usurp a portion of another's possessions.
>
> (Al-Baqarah 2: 188)

There it goes even further and says first of all don't cheat people out of their money, don't scam people out of their money. We'll deal with that in this reminder in some depth. The literal wording is, don't consume the monies of each other using falsehood. That's the literal translation, right? But there it says and don't try to reel in rulers using your money. Literally, now I will repeat myself: don't try to reel in the government, the governor, the chancellor, the council man, don't try to reel them in with your money so that a group of you can eat the rest of the people's money. You know what it's talking about? It's talking about: when business gets involved with politics, corruption happens. So the very wealthy, the business institutions can eventually have politicians in their pockets. And when they do, the one who doesn't have a lot of financial strength, the average citizen, is the one that's going to be paying the price.

In this way big business can actually rob people of their money in collaboration with a government while people sleep. They don't have to bust into their homes and take their money. They can do it while they are sleeping, they can do it through regulation, they can do it with all kinds of loopholes around the law and most people won't even know. And it's incredible that when I discuss this right now, it sounds like I'm talking about contemporary politics but this is something Allah talked about a millennium and a half ago.

Let the Muslim community look, first of all; don't try to scam people out of money and don't get politicians involved in your shady dealings. You're starting a community and when you start a community obviously there's going to be businesses that are going to be established. You're going to have to have economic dealings with each other. Somebody's going to open up a store, somebody's going to open up a chop shop. There are going to be people in different businesses and you are going to have to have dealings with each other of a financial nature. Make sure those are right first. Can you imagine, in its earlier revelation the Qur'an did not come and tell us: by the way make sure when you see someone, say salaam to them. Those are all important things and those are the things we think are Islamic rulings, but what Allah calls Islamic rulings first is actually financial regulation. It's incredible to me. *Lā ta'kulā amwālakum baynakum bi-l-bāṭil*. Then He adds a clause, He says: *illā an takūn tijāratan ʿan tarāḍin minkum*—unless it's a transaction in which both of you are in complete agreement. So, it doesn't matter what business you go into, whatever legitimate business you're doing, make sure between the seller and the buyer there is absolutely clear, crystal clear understanding of the agreement that you have gotten involved with. So now we can think about our times, what is Allah saying to us. This was for them back then; what is Allah saying for us.

You walk into a car dealership, guys trying to sell you a car, obviously a salesperson wants to make his sale so he wants to hide the flaws of his used car and he wants to highlight the benefits: 'Look at the colour; look at the shine on this thing'. He won't talk to you about the transmission, conveniently, because he knows it's got some accidents in its past and so on. And you say, 'Can I see the Carfax?' And he says, 'No, what do you need the Carfax for? Let me tell you. Let me give you a deal, I'm in a good mood today man. I like you, I like your hat. So I'm gonna knock off a thousand dollars'.

You know what he is doing? This is exactly what Allah is talking about: this kind of dealing.

Now if you're a salesman, watch out! Because when you're in the sales business sometimes you'll do anything you can to get the sale. You'll say anything you can, to get somebody to sign off and of course we have this incredible thing nowadays, so you have this contract between you and me. Say I've bought a car and there are eighty-five pages of fine print, the entire point of which is to protect the seller against the buyer. There are probably a lot of things in there that if you actually understood, then you would never have signed that paper. Guess why it's in such a small font? Guess why it's in such legal jargon? The point of it is so that people don't have transparency in their dealings.

I'll give you another example of just how businesses do this. You go to a commercial building and you want to rent an office. Our lease is ten dollars a square foot, even though that is a thing of the past, we don't get ten dollars a square foot anymore. So you get ten dollars a square foot and the contract is for four years. You get an email in two years, 'The prices have gone up. We have raised your rent to twelve dollars'. You'll say, 'Wait, we signed a contract. You said ten. What's going on here?' 'Oh, the fine print said based on market fluctuation, on page 7, line 52.' If you find yourself a microscope, you can zoom in enough and you will find the text says we might pull the rug from underneath your feet whenever we feel like it. This is: *illā an takūn tijārah ʿan tarāḍin minkum*—except if it is a transaction that is mutually agreed upon by both sides.

I'm not talking about just scamming businesses here; I'm talking about ourselves. Many of you are professionals, and given the track record of the Muslim community in the US, many of you are probably in the technology industry. So you are contractors, you are programmers, you are consultants, you are network administrators, some of you are accountants, some of you are physicians. Let's just say you're a programmer, or a contractor, your boss is not hovering over your head 24/7. You walk in, you have a lot of independence, you're just given a task; finish this task and report it back to me, right? And sometimes you can finish your task in twenty minutes. You've got seven hours and forty minutes left to chill that day. So what are you supposed to do?

Some of you, you know what you do? You start listening to Qur'an recitation at the office on YouTube, many companies have blocked YouTube on their corporate machines. Thank God for 4G on your phone now, right? So you're just doing that at work, but you know what? You are being paid to do work. We think that when we are at the office that is between us and the employer. Allah is saying, No that's my business too. How do you deal with your boss? Because this is a *tijārah* too; it's a business too. If you've got no work to do, then go over to your manager and say, 'Listen, I've got nothing to do. I need that off my conscience. If it's okay for me to do nothing right now and still be paid, fine. But I need you to know that, so we are both clear'.

Sometimes you are part of an organization that sells services to another company. They say, 'We'll provide a contract to you, if you sign off for us we can finish this project in six months'. So you have a contract that we are going to finish this job within six months, and you have the wherewithal to finish it in two months. But if you finish it in two months you can't bill them by the hour can you? You can't milk every last penny you can? So you stall it. And even if you finish your work you take it to your manager and he says, 'Just relax man, it's okay, we got time, because we got to bill this thing out.' This is an unethical business practice and you should call it out. You can't just be complacent, as a Muslim, in that situation; you actually have to call it out. We can't stand idly by when people are cheating other people with money and we know about it. You cannot get around the idea by 'everybody's doing it, what can I do?' Everybody does that, you can't. You and I can't; we are people of conscience. We have to answer to a much higher authority, so we have to have a higher level of conscience in our business dealings.

Similarly those of you that are employers and have employees, you have people that work for you. Make sure there is a clear understanding about what their job description is, what is expected of them, what is voluntary and what is paid for, and don't put undue pressure on them. Salary and things like that should be clear, absolutely crystal clear, there should be no surprises. This is the beginnings of a Muslim community, can you imagine. The first thing Allah talks about—take care of business. You know why? Because when you don't take care of business, all kinds of corruption enters into a society that aren't limited to business alone. When people don't worry about how they are making a buck, then they lose their moral compass and then they stop caring about the other; because when you care about the other you can't get away with doing what you do, you have to kill your conscience, little by little.

This is why the very next words in the *āyah* are: *wa-lā taqtulū anfusakum*—and don't kill each other. What is Allah saying? When financial corruption goes rampant, you will find in a society that heinous crimes also rise. Financial corruption leads to other types of crime. *Subḥān Allāh*! That is what Allah is preventing us from—*wa-lā taqtulū anfusakum.*

وَمَن يَفْعَلْ ذَٰلِكَ عُدْوَٰنًا وَظُلْمًا فَسَوْفَ نُصْلِيهِ نَارًا ۚ وَكَانَ
ذَٰلِكَ عَلَى ٱللَّهِ يَسِيرًا ﴿٣٠﴾

(النساء ٤ : ٣٠)

And whoever does this by way of transgression and injustice We shall surely cast him into the Fire; that indeed is quite easy for Allah.

(Al-Nisā' 4: 30)

'And whoever does that out of animosity and wrong doing, [in other words commits murder, or does something that leads to murder,] then We will throw them into the fire and that's easy for Allah to do.' Now why would Allah use such harsh language? Allah is not even talking about 'disbelievers' being thrown into the fire. Allah is saying in the beginning: *Yā ayyuhā alladhīna āmanū*—'Those of you who believe', when you become corrupt I have no problem throwing you also. Don't just wear your faith on your sleeve. Don't just call yourself a Muslim and not represent any of its teachings. You're not going to get away with that. This faith of ours isn't just a declaration, it has to be a lifestyle choice. It has to be a way we do business; it has to be a way in which we deal with each other. *Subḥān Allāh*, it's very powerful.

Now I come to the last *āyah* that I wanted to share with you, but before I do, one more beautiful thing, why did Allah give us these regulations anyway? It's the *āyah* before that I didn't even share with you where He says:

يُرِيدُ ٱللَّهُ أَن يُخَفِّفَ عَنكُمْ ۚ وَخُلِقَ ٱلْإِنسَٰنُ ضَعِيفًا ﴿٢٨﴾
(النساء ٤ : ٢٨)

Allah wants to lighten your burdens, for man was created weak.

(Al-Nisā' 4: 28)

'Allah wants to lighten your burden for you, and the human being was created weak.' I am giving you these principles because if you abide by them you will have an easier life. Here you are thinking if you can make an extra buck, by hook or by crook, that you will have an easier life, but Allah is saying let me tell you: when you make that money in the wrong way, it will come back to haunt you eventually. You'll pay the price for it, maybe in your personal life, in your family life because that money is cursed. It's cursed.

And by the way when Muslims earn money from questionable sources, and then we feel guilty, and we donate to the masjid a part of it. Because we feel guilty. So the guy's running a liquor store—absolutely haram—with a lotto machine on top, right? And he's got the *Āyat al-Kursī* behind the cash register, so everything should be okay. Well, it's not okay. He's running this liquor store and he feels guilty, so he comes in Ramadan and drops a ten thousand dollar cheque to the masjid. That money is dirty and when that money goes into the masjid, into building the walls of that masjid, to cleaning the carpet of that masjid, you shouldn't be surprised that years down the line there are fights happening inside that masjid, and nobody is showing up, and there are all kinds of quarrels, and people don't like each other, and there is all this tension and, and....

Why? because good money comes with *barakah*, good money comes with blessings and bad money comes with *laʿnah*. It's cursed. It has no *barakah* in it, nothing good comes of it. Nothing good can come from something that is evil to begin with; you cannot eat something that is not good for you and expect good results, right? You cannot put poison in your mouth and expect to get healthy; you can't do it, it doesn't make any sense. The world of *īmān* is like that too. You cannot earn something haram, something questionable, and put it to something good and expect good things will happen; they won't. It doesn't work that way, that's not Allah's law—*subḥān Allāh*!

So now this last *āyah*—such a beautiful *āyah*—if the ummah understood this *āyah*, if we just contemplated this *āyah*, we'd be a lot better off than we are now.

إِن تَجْتَنِبُواْ كَبَآئِرَ مَا تُنْهَوْنَ عَنْهُ نُكَفِّرْ عَنكُمْ سَيِّـَٔاتِكُمْ
وَنُدْخِلْكُم مُّدْخَلًا كَرِيمًا ﴿٣١﴾

(النساء ٤ : ٣١)

But if you avoid the major sins which you have been forbidden, We shall remit your (trivial) offences, and cause you to enter an honourable abode.

(Al-Nisā' 4: 31)

Allah says: If you people can, side-step, avoid, get away from the most grievous sins, the most egregious sins, the major sins that you're being prohibited from—*kabā'ir*, the plural of *kabīrah*, is used in the Qur'an for major sins like murder or blasphemy, saying inappropriate things about Allah, *kufr*. These are major sins but which major sin did Allah highlight before even talking about *kabā'ir*? Only two of them: financial dealings and murder. Meaning how you deal with each other is a pretty big deal to Allah. He says if you can avoid this—*in tajtanibū kabā'ir mā tunhawna ʿanhu*—if you can avoid the major transgressions that you're being forbidden from—*nukaffir ʿankum sayyi'ātikum*—He will then, in that case, bury away from you your other sins.

Look, we're all human beings you're going to wake up late for *ṣalāh* one day—it's going to happen. You're going to lose your temper one day and say things you shouldn't have said; you're going to get into a fight eventually with someone, some quarrel; it's going to happen. Your tongue is going to slip and you're going to say something about someone you shouldn't have said, maybe even behind their back. Maybe you're not going to be super honest one day and you're going to lie. We're going to make mistakes. These are *sayyi'āt*, these are sins, evil deeds that all of us commit, we are all human beings, none of us are angels; we're not perfect. Allah says if you can watch out for the big stuff, lead a good life and especially watch out for the big sins, I'll help you take care of the little stuff.

Don't get overworked about the little things. One day you missed a prayer and you're just falling into depression like: '*Astaghfir Allāh*, I'm so burning in *Jahannam* because...'. No, no, no, calm down. Allah will take care of once-in-a-while mistakes you just make sure you're not doing the major sins. You know what has happened in the ummah? Why am I highlighting this? We have flipped this equation, we have turned this equation on its head. So you know what we do? The way we earn money, forget about it! The way we deal with each other, forget it! But man when it comes to the little things! You will question other Muslims; you will investigate the halal restaurant with twenty searches, and then go to the town records and find out where they are slaughtering their meat. But where you earn your money, you won't even think about—*subḥān Allāh*!

I'm not saying that halal and haram is a small thing, what I am saying is there is a perspective. And the perspective is, the first thing you need to worry about is how are you earning your money? That's first. Second, are you hurting other people? Then it's the other regulations. You've gone to the masjid, and maybe you come from a part of the world where the *kufi* on your head is really important to you. So you see a person praying next to you and he's not wearing a *kufi*, and you say: '*Astaghfir Allāh*, he's praying without a *kufi*, his *ṣalāh* won't even get accepted,' because it's really important to you. You know what? It's important to you, but Allah (*ʿazza wa-jall*) gave us priorities. He gave us priorities, you can't make up your own; you and I have to stick to Allah's priorities. If we did that, we'd be a lot better off. Dealing with each other would become a lot easier. How we treat each other would become a lot better if we focused on the major sins and staying away from them.

Just a little comment about *ijtināb*, the word *ijtināb* that's used in the *āyah*—*in tajtanibū*—comes from the word *janb*, and *janb* actually means 'side'. In the Qur'an when Allah talks about speaking nicely to people, He says *wa-l-ṣāḥib bi-l-janb*. Even when you are travelling, and somebody is sitting next to you—like there is an *āyah* in the Qur'an about the guy sitting next to you in the train, or the plane, or the bus, or at the terminal at the airport, the guy sitting next to you. Be nice to them too. Don't pretend they don't exist. Be courteous to them. Even that's mentioned. The word *ijtināb*, to avoid, is actually mentioned as opposed to *al-ibtiʿād ʿan shay'*—to stay away, far away from something. It's mentioned because don't ever think that major sins are so far away from me—I am so protected with my code of righteousness that they'll never touch me. Actually they are right next to you and you have to go out of your way to side-step them.

Literally *ijtināb* is to side-step something that is right there next to you. It's right in your face. So the potential for us to do some pretty big mistakes in life is always there. It's a prevalent, living, immediate danger that we have to look out for. None of us can be self-righteous and say, 'I would never do such a thing! I'm not even in the danger of ever doing such a thing!' No, no, no, actually we are, we're just not sensitive enough. And maybe we're sensitive about the wrong things. We are overly sensitive about the wrong things.

So, let me put everything in balance before I conclude my reminder, *in shā' Allāh taʿālā*. As I said, how we earn our money, how we spend our money, how we deal in business with each other that's a priority in our religion. Dealing with each other with courtesy and respect are priorities in our religion. But that does not mean that everything else about the Shariah is irrelevant. It does not mean that halal meat is irrelevant. It doesn't mean that the *Sunnah* prayers is irrelevant. It doesn't mean that all this other stuff that you have learned about your religion is irrelevant. But you know what those things are? First of all the *Sharʿī* things—the halal and the haram—are a major priority in your personal life. That's not for you to judge others; that's for you, yourself. Everything beyond that is there so that I can improve myself as a Muslim. Not so that I can label others and say, 'Look at this guy, look at where his pants are going'. 'Look at this one, look at how he prayed.' 'Look at that guy, he doesn't even have a beard.' 'Look at that girl her hijab is all messed up'; etc, etc. No, no, no. The *aḥkām* of the *dīn* first and foremost are for you, yourself.

They are not for you to label other people as to where they stand. That's something that their family has to do. That's something that their community has to do, and if you can't say something good, then don't say anything. You don't know what people are going through; I don't know what people are going through; you can't pass judgement on people. And I tell you, the kind of person that makes it very easy for themselves to pass judgement on others has a certain psychology. It's the kind of person that is probably involved in some pretty major stuff themselves, and they turn a blind eye to it. And when you become blind to yourself, you develop an extra sharp focus on others.

You already graduated from the school of righteousness, right? Since you don't need to turn back and check on yourself anymore, now your attention can be turned to everybody else. That's the problem. This is: *in tajtanibū kabā'ir mā tunhawna ʿanhu nukaffir ʿankum sayyi'ātikum*—I'll forgive your other sins, I'll overlook them. It's not an open licence for you and me to sin, but Allah is effectively saying: 'Look, the big ones I will not forgive; I will not forgive. The smaller mistakes you make—by mistake not purposefully, because another *āyah* in the Qur'an talks about people that make mistakes purposefully—but by mistake if you fall into sin I will forgive you so long as you ask me for forgiveness sincerely'. *Subḥān Allāh*!

This is the gift of the Qur'an. It puts things in perspective, it gives us a sense of priority. What should I worry about and what shouldn't I worry about. What should I make a big deal of in my life, and what can maybe take to the side, and I can work on it, little by little by little. Like if somebody wants to, for example, introduce the *sunnah* prayers in their life. Or maybe for some of you the *sunnah* prayers are hard, you're barely making the *farḍ*. Okay, introduce one *sunnah*; just the Fajr. Keep that up for a week or two, then add another *sunnah*. You don't have to do all of it at once, you can build. You can get better little by little by little. But when it comes to the *kabā'ir* you don't say, 'Well I'm earning haram right now, but I'm little by little getting out of it'. You can't do that. 'I'm hurting people but I'm slowly trying to stop.' No, no, no, there's no slowly, that stuff you have to let go cold turkey. You've got to make a decision, because that is not something that Allah (*ʿazza wa-jall*) is willing to tolerate.

I pray that we become people that stay far away from the *kabā'ir*—the major mistakes. I pray the way that we earn our money and we spend our money is pleasing to Allah (*ʿazza wa-jall*); and that it is governed by principles of fairness and clarity. I pray that, for those of us who are in businesses, Allah (*ʿazza wa-jall*) gives us the ability, the moral strength, the conviction to be able to engage in fair, clear and open business transactions. I pray that the money that is donated to all *masājid* is good, pure, halal money; that the *barakah* of that money can show, *in shā' Allāh taʿālā*, in the activities, in the community building that comes as a result of it.

CHAPTER 7

Money Matters

In this reminder, *in shā' Allāh ta'ālā*, I'll share with you some thoughts about *āyāt* that belong to *Sūrat al-Isrā'*. These are a handful of *āyāt* in which Allah (*'azza wa-jall*) gives us some guidance about how we should think about our money and how we should think about shopping and spending.

The first *āyah* I want to share with you is the twenty-fifth *āyah* of the surah where Allah (*'azza wa-jall*) says:

رَّبُّكُمْ أَعْلَمُ بِمَا فِي نُفُوسِكُمْ ۚ إِن تَكُونُوا صَالِحِينَ فَإِنَّهُ
كَانَ لِلْأَوَّابِينَ غَفُورًا ﴿٢٥﴾

(الإسراء ١٧ : ٢٥)

Your Lord is best aware of what is in your hearts. If you are righteous, He will indeed forgive those who relent and revert (to serving Allah).

(Al-Isrā' 17: 25)

Rabbukum aʿlam bi-mā fī nufūsikum—Allah knows better, your Master is more knowledgeable, more aware with regards to what you have inside of yourselves. So before Allah even gives us the *aḥkām*, Allah tells us He knows better what we have inside of us. This is actually an *ishārah*—a hint—that whatever Allah is about to teach us now, can only be checked by you; yourself. In other words I will not be able to come and correct you, and you will not be able to come and correct me directly. This is something that we are going to have to figure out for ourselves, it is a matter of personal conscience and personal morality.

Someone who does not watch over themselves carefully, does not do *muḥāsabah* of themselves, they are not going to be able to live by the instructions that are about to be given, and have already been given, in this surah. Allah says: *Rabbukum aʿlam bi-mā fī nufūsikum in takūnū ṣāliḥīn*—if in fact you are good, if in fact you are righteous, then Allah knows that better—*fa-innahū kāna li-l-awwābīna ghafūrā*—for those who keep coming back to Allah in repentance. Just as we have the word *tawwāb*, similarly we have the word *awwāb*, people who come back to Allah sincerely. They feel bad about what they have done and they keep recognizing that they've made a mistake and they keep coming back, for those people Allah is exceedingly forgiving. Inside the word *awwāb* there is also a lesson—the idea that we are never going to stop making mistakes; there is always going to be something we could have done better. We constantly have to recognize that in ourselves—I have to recognize that in myself, you have to recognize that in yourself, and then we have to keep making *istaghfār* to Allah for the shortcomings that we have. We have to be constantly aware of our own flaws. Instead of waiting for somebody else to point out what's wrong with me I should be the first one to point out what's wrong with myself, and constantly acknowledge that before Allah.

It is a beautiful thing actually and it's directly connected with the perfection of Allah—the only one who is perfect is Allah, which means all of us have some flaw. We're always going to have flaws and we're never going to be done with our mistakes. It's never going to happen. So the fact that we recognize our mistakes and then ask Allah to cover up those mistakes—this is the idea of *maghfirah*: to cover things up, to cover the flaws. If you see a crack in the ground, you cover it with cement or something this is literally the idea of *maghfirah*. The fact that we do this is an acknowledgement that we are imperfect and also an acknowledgement that only Allah is perfect. People who cease to recognize that in themselves—may Allah not make us from them—people who just don't actually think about what's wrong with them and what they could make better about themselves, they have actually forgotten about the perfection of Allah.

وَءَاتِ ذَا ٱلْقُرْبَىٰ حَقَّهُۥ وَٱلْمِسْكِينَ وَٱبْنَ ٱلسَّبِيلِ وَلَا تُبَذِّرْ تَبْذِيرًا ﴿٢٦﴾

(الإسراء ١٧ : ٢٦)

Give to the near of kin his due, and also to the needy and the wayfarer. Do not squander your wealth wastefully.

(Al-Isrā' 17: 26)

Now, Allah gives us advice about how to spend our money, He says: *wa-āti dhā al-qurbā ḥaqqahū*—and give to the one who possesses closeness—not *dhawī al-qurbā* but *dhā al-qurbā*—give the one relative, his right. Allah is not making us think about all of our relatives at the same time, it is as though Allah is saying, consider each one of them individually.

What happens in a lot of families? A lot of families, if you're an average family, then you have some fight in your family. Some uncle you don't like, some cousin you don't get along with, some brother that you had a problem with or whatever. Then if somebody needs help, you think of helping the people that you get along with but you don't think of helping the people that you had a fight with. We skip them. 'That uncle? No, no, no! He's not getting anything. Zakat? I'll give it to some other place. Some *ṣadaqah* I'll give it to my *khala*, but my *chacha*!? Forget about him. No, no, no. I hate that guy.'

Allah is telling us: actually, if they are close to you and Allah gave them that relationship to you—*wa-ulū āl-arḥām baʿḍuhum awlā bi-baʿḍin fī Kitāb Allāh* (*al-Aḥzāb* 33: 6)—the people that are connected to you by the womb of a mother; maybe you're connected by your grandmother, maybe your connected by your mother or your father, these are connections of the womb. If you have that connection then you have to consider each and every one of them. If they're in need—whether you like them or not, whether you had a fight with them or not—if they deserve your help then you have to give it to them. And Allah here in this incredible *āyah* did not say: *wa-āti dhā al-qurbā* and then after that *amwālak* or *mālak*; He said, *ḥaqqahū*—give him what he deserves. Give him his right!

In other words the money sitting in my pocket, that should be given to my family members that are in need, is actually not my money according to the Qur'an; it's their money, that I'm holding—it's their right. Just like when you hire someone to do a job for you, after they finish their job the money you had agreed to pay them, if you haven't paid them it yet, and it's in your pocket, it's still not your money. It's actually their money and you have to give it to them. You can't think of it as, 'Oh, I'm just going to go shopping with this cash'. You can't. You owe it to someone else. That mentality has to permeate, has to be internalized by the Muslims, that for our close relatives, the ones that need help, that's actually their money. What we have in our pocket is actually their money. It's in our account, we login and see it in our account, but it's actually not ours; It's his right—*ḥaqqahū*—according to Allah.

When you owe someone money, you are quick to pay it, especially if it's a higher authority. You owe the government taxes, you pay it quickly. You owe the electricity company money or there are going to cut the electricity, you'll pay the bill quickly. When you owe something and you know that there are going to be consequences, you and I will pay it quickly. Allah (*ʿazza wa-jall*) is now the authority behind the close relative. The close relative may not have any authority, as a matter of fact, if he deserves zakat and he or she deserves *ṣadaqah*, then they are not financially capable. This means they are most likely not in a position of authority; but now their authority is validated by Allah. Allah is the authority that is saying you better give them their right.

Wa-l-miskīn—then on top of that, the second is *al-miskīn*. *Miskīn* is a combination of two words *masaka* and *sakana* in Arabic. It's formulated by both of those words together. It means people that are stuck in a situation. *Miskīn* does not mean poor people, there are other words for that in the Arabic language, for example *fuqarā'*. *Miskīn* is a deeper concept. The idea of a *miskīn* is someone who is not able to help themselves, in their financial situation, their political situation or whatever problem. For example, if somebody is a cab driver and he makes his money, provides for his family, by driving a cab. But his eyes become weak or he has to go for surgery and he is legally considered blind. Now he can't drive the cab anymore. It's the only job he had, and now he's stuck. He's not a beggar, he's not a poor person, but he is stuck in that situation. You have people for example that have reached an age where they have retired but their retirement savings are not enough for them. They're not even able to get the groceries, they're stuck. They are not of the age where they can go and get another job—they have a health condition, they have something else going on in their life, they're not able to do it. You have single mothers; they have children that they have to take care of and they can't afford day care. They can't go get a job because they have to take care of their kids and there's no family, no other support that can help them. These are the people that are called *miskīn*—they're stuck. They can't help themselves. Literally, just from every angle, they're just caught, and they don't know what to do.

Allah says take care of those people. And, by the way, it's an extension, so the first people we look for are within our own family. Then we identify people who are in that situation in our community. But the problem is how are you going to know? How am I going to know that in the city of Irving, Dallas, in a particular zip code, in this neighbourhood, there's some family who has that problem. How are we supposed to know? If we don't get to know one another and we don't make the effort to know each other's families. If we don't just give salaams to each other in a grumpy way after *Jumuʿah* and walk away, but actually make friends with each other—our families get to know one another. Then we really become a community, and when someone has a problem, they don't have to go begging, they don't have to hold their hand out—we would know already. We would know somebody lost a job. We would know somebody got diagnosed with a disease. We would know somebody has too many medical expenses. We would know those things and we'd help them privately, right? This is the idea of a community. That's what we're supposed to do.

We cannot live by this *āyah* if we don't have the idea of *taḥābbū* whereby the Prophet (*ṣallā Allāh ʿalayhi wa-sallam*) said—you're not going to have *īmān* until you love one another. We have to love one another. And the idea of *afshū al-salām* in that same hadith—spread the salaam. Why spread the salaam? It's not just: '*Al-salām ʿalaykum*'. '*Wa-ʿalaykum al-salām.*' Okay, you get your shoes, I get my shoes and we're out of here. That's not the only salaam. Salaam means you introduce yourself to each other. You get to know one another. Then you get to know who the *masākīn* are.

The next idea is: *wa-ibn al-sabīl*. The one they call: 'the son of the path', that's literally the term used in the Arabic language. The idea of son is the idea of someone who's associated with something. In other words it's the one who's constantly travelling; the one who can't afford to live for long in one place. Like in ancient societies the Bedouins used to travel all the time. They could not stay in one place for long; they had to keep moving along. One kind of person this includes is the *musāfir*—someone who is travelling and going through the city or whatever. But the other category of *wa-ibn al-sabīl* is people who can't afford stable housing. They're living in a motel, then they're living in somebody's house, then they're living somewhere else, then somewhere else; because they are in such a dire situation they are not able to stay in one place. They don't have a permanent home, they can call their own. We have to identify those kinds of people, and if there's an opportunity, to help them.

For example, if you have a family member who lives in say, North Carolina, who calls you and says, 'Listen, we're having a bit of a situation. Can the children stay with you for a few weeks?' It's inconvenient because you have your own family, you have your own things to take care of and they're saying can we come over for a few weeks? Actually we are supposed to understand that, that is their right. That your house, the house that you live in, is actually not only your house; when they are in need, a piece of it is for them, according to Allah. This is their *ḥaqq* and we have to give it. We can't say, 'Oh, well, you know, it's a busy time right now. I don't really know if I can do that. I can give you some phone numbers for local hotels'. No, no, no! We have to have the attitude of giving.

Now Allah says all of this: *wa-āti dhā al-qurbā ḥaqqahū wa-l-miskīn wa-ibn al-sabīl*—but the ending of this *āyah* is remarkably a completely different subject. He says: *wa-lā tubadhdhir tabdhīrā*—don't spend frivolously, and don't go out of your way to spend wastefully. Let me explain these words a little bit: the first thing that comes out of the ground is called *al-badhr*. In other words, when a farmer plants a seed and a plant starts coming out, they have to wait a long time before it's fully grown. If it's just come out a little bit, it's premature. It's not ready, if you cut it right now, there's no benefit. Similarly there are some people, as soon as some money comes into their hand, they spend it. As soon as they get their pay cheque, they have to get a new pair of Jordans, or they have to get a big screen TV, or they have to go to a really expensive restaurant.

They spend all their money, every chance they get. Also some linguists comment on the idea of *tabdhīr* as *tafrīq al-māl bi-lā muḥāsabah, yaʿnī isrāfuhū*—you just spread your money in every direction, without any concern. 'Money ain't a thing bro. I got this. It's not a problem.' You walk into an electronics superstore, 'I want the biggest TV you got'. 'That one is $8000.' 'I don't care, put it in. I got this.' You just don't care about how you spend your money.

Now, here it's important that Allah adds: *wa-lā tubadhdhir tabdhīrā*—please listen to this carefully—Allah did not just say, don't spend your money wastefully. He said: don't go out of your way to spend money wastefully. This is the incredible *ḥikmah* of the Qur'an. To some extent, all of us will waste some money, it's inevitable. Taking this to an extreme, for example, Eid comes and you think of buying your wife a new dress or something. She picks out this dress but you're like,' *wa-lā tubadhdhir tabdhīrā*. No, no, no, we're not going to buy that dress'. Or you're about to buy your kids some toys, or get a present for somebody, and you're like, 'No we're not going to do *tabdhīr*'. Or you're about to get a new car and you're like, 'I don't want to do *tabdhīr*. I'll get a 1978 Cutlass Ciera. Anything more than that, I don't need it, it still has four wheels and still goes from point A to point B'. So you're just going to buy yourself a donkey and a cart behind it and that's how you're going to live your life, even if the highway authority has a problem with that.

No, no, no, that's not what the idea of *tabdhīr* is. The idea of *tabdhīr* is that you don't *constantly* go over in spending more than you need to, in things that you need and things you don't need, without any discrimination, all the time. If you develop that habit of constantly spending money without any consideration, any sense of financial responsibility, and you know why this is the case? And, by the way, this is the same *āyah* we haven't even gone to another *āyah* yet. Because if you keep spending your money like that, what are you going to give to your family? What are you going to give to the *miskīn*? What are you going to give to the one that is in a homeless situation, or the traveller? What are you going to give to them? You've got nothing left to give because it all goes into your obsession, into your collection.

It's okay to redecorate your house, it's no problem. It's okay to get a new carpet, no problem. But if you're constantly doing that! *Wa-lā tubadhdhir tabdhīrā*—this is why in the next *āyah* Allah does not say: *Inna alladhīna yubadhdhirūn*—He says: *inna al-mubadhdhirīn*—the *ism faʿil* (active participle) is used—which suggests these are people who do this all the time. They just develop this habit and they do it all the time. What does Allah say about them? It is one of the worst things said in the

Qur'an about people. It is one of the worst labels, ever given, in the entire Qur'an. Allah says:

إِنَّ ٱلْمُبَذِّرِينَ كَانُوٓا۟ إِخْوَٰنَ ٱلشَّيَٰطِينِ ۖ وَكَانَ ٱلشَّيْطَٰنُ لِرَبِّهِۦ كَفُورًا ﴿٢٧﴾

(الإسراء ١٧ : ٢٧)

For those who squander wastefully are Satan's brothers, and Satan is ever ungrateful to his Lord.
(Al-Isrā' 17: 27)

Inna al-mubadhdhirīn kānū ikhwān al-shayāṭīn—the people who spend recklessly all the time, prematurely spending their money, they have been declared the brothers of *shayāṭīn*. They are the brothers of the devils.

Why in the world would these people who spend recklessly be considered brothers of *shayāṭīn*? Let's think about this for a little bit. First and foremost: *al-ʿajalah min al-shayṭān*—rushing comes from *shayṭān*. To begin with the idea of you becoming impulsive and rushing into spending your money, without thinking twice about it, is actually something satanic. Secondly, when you spend a lot of money frivolously on useless things—if people spend tons of money on entertainment, which industry makes a lot of money? You're spending it, you're the customer. You don't make the money it's the entertainment industry that makes the money. So when you spend your money on useless things, useless industries become successful. When you spend your money on wasteful things, the wasteful enterprise, the wasteful corporations, they're the ones that thrive. And when they thrive *shayṭān*'s work succeeds in society. We become part of the machinery of *shayṭān*.

The other part of this, that's really important to understand, *inna al-mubadhdhirīn kānū ikhwān al-shayāṭīn*—Allah tells us Himself: *wa-kāna al-shayṭān li-Rabbihī kafūrā*—please listen to this part very carefully, it's the scariest part. Allah could have told us so many things about *shayṭān* in this *āyah*, but the one thing He told us is that *shayṭān* has always been extremely ungrateful to his Master. Allah mentions his extreme ingratitude. You will notice something about shopaholics, that's what they call them, right? Shopaholics? They shop all the time. They're never done buying shoes. They're never done buying technology. They're never done buying whatever else. They're constantly buying, buying, buying and buying. Guess what? They're never happy. They're never grateful for what they have; their eyes are always on what they don't have. What more can I buy? What more can I acquire? What more can I get? All the time.

In other words, this idea of the constant consumer—you can only be a constant consumer if you're constantly dissatisfied. And dissatisfaction is the exact opposite of gratitude. *Shayṭān* is dissatisfied, he's ungrateful; and so is a *mubadhdhir*. So is someone who spends frivolously all the time. They are never grateful, they are never appreciative. Actually, when that mentality sets in, the only thing they appreciate is what they don't have. They actually don't value what they do have, they only value what they don't have. If they have a really nice car; you sit in their car and say, 'Wow, this is a really nice car', but their eyes are on some other car. 'Well, I was thinking about getting that one.' They could have a really nice house; you go to their house and say, 'Wow, this is an amazing house', but they are like, 'Well, actually I was thinking of moving to a better neighbourhood'. They're looking at a better house; they're looking at another house.

We've turned some of our children into this monster. We buy them one video game, another video game, another, then another, and now they've got a collection. They've got this massive collection. 'Hey, wow, you have that game? And you have that game?' 'Yeah, but I don't have THAT one.' What's really burning their soul right now is that they don't have THAT one. It's the same with the new iPhone culture, 'You have an iPhone 4? *Astaghfir Allāh al-ʿaẓīm*! What kind of a primitive Muslim are you? You don't even have an iPhone 5!' 'You only have an iPhone 5C? Oh, *miskīn*, you don't have a 5S.' Then, even the one that has a 5S is making *du'ā'*, late at night: when is the new iPhone 6 coming out?

The idea of you just constantly being dissatisfied with what you have. It's not enough for you! You want something more, then you want something more, and more after that. It's a constant thing. By the way, human beings have a tendency to want something better. We have that. We're always going to like another car—it's always going to be there. We're always going to drive past a nice neighbourhood and like the neighbourhood, it's natural! You're always going to go to some store and look at some clothes that you cannot afford or didn't buy, but they're nice. We have that inside of us, but the difference between that and a *mubadhdhir* is that the *mubadhdhir* has no brakes. He sees it, he likes it, he gets it. He just gets it. He doesn't think about the consequences. You can like things, but you have to have a sense of limits. Put some brakes on! You don't have to get everything you like! You can learn to be a little more satisfied with what you have. Be happy with what you have. You can spend on things you like, but don't overspend on things you like, because once that becomes an addiction then: *inna al-mubadhdhirīn kānū ikhwān al-shayāṭīn, wa-kāna al-shayṭān li-Rabbihī kafūrā*.

May Allah (*'azza wa-jall*) make us people who are serious about the way they think about their money.

Because the next *āyah* is about money, but I know I'm getting late, I will just share it very quickly with you. Allah describes the scenario of a person who has some money, and then a relative comes to them, or a poor person comes to them, or a neighbour, or a *miskīn* comes to them and asks them for help. Maybe you don't have anything right now. Maybe you've put your money in some investment already, or you barely have enough for yourself, and you're not able to give them anything. Sometimes people ask, and you're not able to give.

وَإِمَّا تُعْرِضَنَّ عَنْهُمُ ٱبْتِغَآءَ رَحْمَةٍ مِّن رَّبِّكَ تَرْجُوهَا فَقُل لَّهُمْ قَوْلًا مَّيْسُورًا ﴿٢٨﴾

(الإسراء ١٧ : ٢٨)

And when you must turn away from them—(that is, from the destitute, the near of kin, the needy, and the wayfarer)—in pursuit of God's Mercy which you expect to receive, then speak to them kindly.

(Al-Isrā' 17: 28)

Wa-immā tu'riḍanna 'anhum—and if you are avoiding those people who are asking you, you're kind of getting away from them because you're embarrased that you don't have anything to give. *Wa-immā tu'riḍanna 'anhum ibtighā' raḥmatin min Rabbika*—you're only avoiding them because you're seeking *raḥmah* from your *Rabb*. What in the world does that mean? There are some people that when somebody comes and asks them they say, 'I don't have anything' in a very harsh tone. For example, the homeless guy at the red light comes to the window, but you say, 'I don't have anything bro, just go to the next car', in a dismissive manner; you push him away like that. No! Allah is saying if they come to you and you try to respectfully avoid them. The way in which you avoid them shows that you yourself are a *faqīr*, you are desperately in need of the *raḥmah* of your *Rabb*. Meaning Allah is watching, even when you say no. This person is a *faqīr* for money, but you are a *faqīr* for the *raḥmah* of Allah. You are bankrupt for the *raḥmah* of Allah. So watch your attitude when you turn someone down.

Wa-immā tuʿriḍanna ʿanhum ibtighāʾ raḥmatin min Rabbika tarjūhā—you are pursuing the *raḥmah* of Allah, the love and care of Allah that you hope for—*fa-qul lahum qawlan maysūrā*: then speak to them in a nice way; let them down easy. Give them a hug; tell them I feel your pain, as soon as I can, I'll try to do whatever I can, but this is a difficult time for me. I can share this meal with you right now but I don't really have anything more. And I feel horrible letting you down. *fa-qul lahum qawlan maysūrā*—speak with them in soft language—*subḥān Allāh*! Because when they came to us, asking us, they were bringing with them the *raḥmah* of Allah. And when we cannot give them anything, then we have to beg for the *raḥmah* of Allah that came and we could not afford it. We could not get it. This is the ultimate *rizq,* the real *rizq* we get is not the things we buy. The real *rizq* we get is the *raḥmah* of Allah and that comes when we give, not when we buy, not when we take. It's actually when we give that we receive the *raḥmah* of Allah.

May Allah (*ʿazza wa-jall*) make us a people that give, especially to the close relatives, to those around us that are stuck in difficult situations, those who are stuck in debt. There are some students that are stuck in debt. They have college loans that they are paying but they can't get out of. There are people in difficult situations like that. May Allah (*ʿazza wa-jall*) give us the ability to help people that are in those kinds of situations. May Allah (*ʿazza wa-jall*) make us of those who do not become from the *mubadhdhirīn,* who are not reckless spenders. May Allah (*ʿazza wa-jall*) put *barakah* and goodness and *faḍl* in all of our *rizq,* all of the provision that He provides us. May He make all of our earnings halal and pure, and may He make it a means by which, not only do we consume halal, but we earn His *raḥmah* and His forgiveness by becoming people of *ṣadaqah.*

PART IV

SOME CONTEMPORARY ISSUES

CHAPTER 8

It's a Girl!

In shā' Allāh in this brief reminder, I would like to share with you something that I feel is timeless. It's something that Allah (*ʿazza wa-jall*) addresses in His book that was not just a problem for ancient Arabs in the desert, but is actually a problem across many societies and it persists even today. The unfortunate reality is that the evil that is being addressed in the *āyāt* of *Sūrat al-Naḥl*—the sixteenth surah—the evil that's being talked about has somehow survived even among Muslims. Even though Allah (*ʿazza wa-jall*) addressed this disease as a disease that the people of *shirk* used to have, for some reason or another, *shayṭān* has been successful in maintaining this virus across the generations in many lands, in many families, in many cultures among the Muslims.

But the way I want to discuss this, *in shā' Allāh taʿālā*, first and foremost, is how the *āyāt* after the subject matter are. Meaning, I am going to begin, not from the *āyāt* where the subject begins but, where the *āyāt* conclude. Allah (*ʿazza wa-jall*) says:

وَيَجْعَلُونَ لِلَّهِ مَا يَكْرَهُونَ ... ﴿٦٢﴾
(النحل ١٦ : ٦٢)

They assign to Allah what they dislike for themselves ...

(Al-Naḥl 16: 62)

They attribute to Allah what they hate themselves. They give to Allah what they hate themselves. The Quraysh used to have this practice where they had idols but they believed in Allah too, there are *āyāt* in *Sūrat Luqmān* that make that clear.

وَلَئِن سَأَلْتَهُم مَّنْ خَلَقَ ٱلسَّمَـٰوَٰتِ وَٱلْأَرْضَ لَيَقُولُنَّ ٱللَّهُ ... ﴿٢٥﴾
(لقمان ٣١ : ٢٥)

If you were to ask them: "Who created the heavens and the earth?" they will certainly reply: "Allah."...

(Luqmān 31: 25)

'If you asked them who created the skies and the earth even they will tell you it is Allah.' But at the same time they had other gods and other priorities. Within what they used to eat, for example, they would take the best of the meat for themselves and take the leftovers and leave that as a dedication for the idols, or leave it for Allah. So they would basically give to Allah what they don't want for themselves.

Similarly, of course, the Arabs had a tradition of not wanting daughters, they didn't like daughters. They thought having a daughter is a humiliation, but they had no problem attributing daughters to Allah. Allah (*'azza wa-jall*) talks about that in the Qur'an:

أَفَأَصْفَىٰكُمْ رَبُّكُم بِٱلْبَنِينَ وَٱتَّخَذَ مِنَ ٱلْمَلَٰٓئِكَةِ إِنَٰثًا ... ﴿٤٠﴾

(الإسراء ١٧ : ٤٠)

> What, has your Lord favoured you with sons and has taken for Himself daughters from among the angels? ...
>
> (Al-Isrā' 17: 40)

You prefer sons for yourselves but somehow Allah took angels as daughters for Himself. Where do you come up with these ridiculous themes? You don't want that for yourselves. Behind it is a mentality and the mentality is that Allah will be happy so long as you give Him something. Just give Him something; but most of your life and everything that you work for and your priorities are for yourself. You have to live for yourself, not for Allah.

It's like the fact that nobody likes paying taxes and they like to get away with giving as little tax as possible. Well giving zakat to Allah, giving *ṣadaqah* to Allah, giving dedication or devotion to Allah, even giving time to Allah is something you just have to do, so that you can live the rest of your life for yourself. That is the sick mentality that these people had and that is what Allah comments on when He says they give to Allah what they don't like for themselves.

وَيَجْعَلُونَ لِلَّهِ مَا يَكْرَهُونَ وَتَصِفُ أَلْسِنَتُهُمُ ٱلْكَذِبَ أَنَّ لَهُمُ ٱلْحُسْنَىٰ لَا جَرَمَ أَنَّ لَهُمُ ٱلنَّارَ وَأَنَّهُم مُّفْرَطُونَ ﴿٦٢﴾
(النحل ١٦ : ٦٢)

> They assign to Allah what they dislike for themselves and their tongues utter a sheer lie in stating that a happy state awaits them. Without doubt the Fire awaits them and it is to it that they shall be hastened.
>
> (Al-Naḥl 16: 62)

They'll give Allah the minimum amount of time, they'll give Allah the least, the worst of their dedications or their charities etc. 'And their tongues are very eloquent at coming up with lies.' Allah could have just said: *yaqūlūn al-kadhib*—'they tell lies'; but He says *taṣif alsinatuhum al-kadhib. Al-waṣf* in Arabic is the ability to describe something and not everybody is good at describing things. So Allah is talking about people that are eloquent. Then He uses the word *alsinah*; and *alsinah* (lit. 'tongues') you'll find in the Qur'an is used for people who are very good with their words. So they have these flowery, elaborate explanations of lies that they beautify for themselves and the people around them.

Now what is that lie—*anna lahum al-ḥusnā*—that they will have the absolute best. That somehow, whatever little they've given to Allah is such a big deal that, they should expect from Allah the best of the best of the best. This is their lie. *La jarama anna lahum al-nār*—there's no doubt about it, these people, all they have is the fire—*wa-annahum mufraṭūn*—and they are going to be stuffed and then stuffed further inside the fire. Not only *mudkhalūn*—they are going to be entered. *Ifrāṭ* in Arabic is to go beyond the limit. It's one thing to get pushed into Hellfire, it's another to get pushed and then shoved even further. That's *mufraṭūn*. These are very serious *āyāt*, and one of the few places in the Qur'an, where Allah (*ʿazza wa-jall*) swears by Himself. Allah (*ʿazza wa-jall*) swears on serious occasions, it's not something small when Allah Himself swears. But even more serious when He swears by Himself. In Arabic when you swear by Allah, you normally say *wa-Llāhi*. But if that is not enough and you have to go out of your way, you say *ta-Llāhi*, the *tā'* is used.

تَٱللَّهِ لَقَدْ أَرْسَلْنَآ إِلَىٰٓ أُمَمٍ مِّن قَبْلِكَ فَزَيَّنَ لَهُمُ ٱلشَّيْطَـٰنُ أَعْمَـٰلَهُمْ فَهُوَ وَلِيُّهُمُ ٱلْيَوْمَ وَلَهُمْ عَذَابٌ أَلِيمٌ ﴿٦٣﴾

(النحل ١٦ : ٦٣)

By Allah, (O Muḥammad), We sent Messengers to other communities before you but Satan made their evil deeds attractive to them (so they paid no heed to the call of the Messengers). The same Satan is their patron today and they are heading towards a painful chastisement.

(Al-Naḥl 16: 63)

In this next *āyah* we find: *ta-Llāhi laqad arsalnā ilā umam min qablik*—I swear by Allah, Allah Himself is swearing by Himself, We had sent messengers to many nations before them too. But what did *shayṭān* do with all of them? *fa-zayyana lahum al-shayṭān aʿmālahum*—*shayṭān* somehow beautified their deeds to them. They did evil things, but they were so convinced that they are doing some great thing, or that this is the way you are supposed to think or that this is the way you're supposed to behave. *Fa-huwa waliyyuhum al-yawm wa-lahum ʿadhāb alīm*—he (*shayṭān*) is their friend then, on that day, on the day of judgement, that's their friend. That's who they listened to. That's the one whose dictates and whose beautification they accepted. These are some very harsh *āyāt* about people who have the wrong kind of mindset. These are the concluding *āyāt*; these are not the *āyāt* where this conversation begins. So I want to now take you back and tell you where this passage begins.

وَيَجْعَلُونَ لِلَّهِ ٱلْبَنَٰتِ سُبْحَٰنَهُۥ ۙ وَلَهُم مَّا يَشْتَهُونَ ﴿٥٧﴾
(النحل ١٦ : ٥٧)

They assign daughters to Allah—glory be to Him—whereas they assign to themselves what they truly desire!

(Al-Naḥl 16: 57)

Allah (*ʿazza wa-jall*) says: 'They attribute—they put in place for Allah (*subḥānahū wa-taʿālā*) daughters. How perfect He is above that allegation', and then He says: *wa-lahum mā yashtahūn*—but they get to have what they love having. So they want to give Allah daughters but they love having what? Sons, right? Now listen to this next *āyah*:

وَإِذَا بُشِّرَ أَحَدُهُم بِٱلْأُنثَىٰ ظَلَّ وَجْهُهُۥ مُسْوَدًّا وَهُوَ كَظِيمٌ ﴿٥٨﴾
(النحل ١٦ : ٥٨)

When any of them is told about the birth of a female his face turns dark, and he is filled with suppressed anger.

(Al-Naḥl 16: 58)

'When one of them is given the congratulations of the girl…'. So he is waiting for his wife to deliver the child—there are no sonograms back in the day—and now finally, the baby is born, and he's waiting to hear the news. He was hoping to hear that it's a boy, the midwife comes out and she says, 'It's a girl!' Allah says: *al-unthā—the* girl. Now, in any culture you say *unthā* not *al-unthā*; in other words, you say 'a girl' not 'the girl'. But to Allah (*ʿazza wa-jall*) she is special, so He says *al-unthā* not *wa-idhā bushshira aḥaduhum bi-unthā*. Rather, *bi-l-unthā*. The *al-* is for honouring (*takrīm*). He honours this daughter that's been born. In contrast, the husband's given the news and as soon as he hears it's a girl: *ẓalla wajhuhū muswaddah*—his face turns dark. Allah doesn't say that he said anything yet but you could just see the darkness, the cloud hanging over his face. This is Allah describing a *mushrik* (idolator)! Someone who doesn't believe in Allah! When you don't appreciate a daughter, it's like you're not appreciating your own mother, that's where you came from. And so his face becomes darkened and depressed, and before I even go further, let me highlight that this is supposed to be a disease of the *mushrikūn*. They're supposed to get sad when they hear that a daughter is born; not the believer. Not the believer in this Prophet (*ṣallā Allāh ʿalayhi wa-sallam*).

Do you know how many *aḥadīth* there are—one after another after another after another—about daughters. *Rasūl Allāh* (*ṣallā Allāh ʿalayhi wa-sallam*) made such a big deal out of daughters! It's not a small subject. It's not one hadith or two hadiths. It's hadith after hadith after hadith.

Lā yakūn li-aḥadikum thalāth banāt aw thalāth akhawāt fa-aḥsana ilayhinna illā dakhala al-jannah—'There's not a single one of you that has three daughters or even three sisters and he is good to them; except that he goes into *jannah*.' Your goodness to your daughters will land you in *jannah*. In another hadith it says: *lam ya'idhā*—'he didn't bury her alive', okay, *al-ḥamd li-Llāh* he didn't do that—*wa-lam yu'thir waladahū ʿalayhā*—'and he didn't give preference to his son over his daughter'; that one gets *jannah*. So he didn't compare his daughter to his son. He didn't think having a girl. 'Oh I wish I had a boy, man. I was really looking forward to a boy. What are we going to do? This is such a burden on my family. Now I have to pay for her education and it won't even pay back. She's not even going to get a job and provide for the family. She is going to get married and be somebody else's family, and then we have to pay for the wedding on top of that! All these expenses!' He keeps giving preference to his son or wanting to have a son, even that mentality can be a block for you from getting into *jannah*.

Half these *aḥadīth* are about a direct ticket to *jannah* and the other half of the *aḥadīth* are about how these girls will become a barrier (*satr*) between him and Hellfire. His daughters will be the wall between him and Hell. Allah didn't say that about sons, by the way. He said that about daughters. It's an honour Allah gave to these girls that are born in our households. I'm reminded—I say this often, *al-ḥamd li-Llāh*—Allah has blessed me with four daughters. I'm one over the hadith limit, but I will tell you something: I had two daughters in a row, and then when my third daughter was born I was really happy. And so I got a bunch of doughnuts and I went to the masjid. For 'Ishā', I'm just going to give everybody doughnuts because we had a girl again. This brother came outside the masjid and he said 'Oh doughnuts? What happened? Good news?' I said 'Yeah, it's a girl' and he said, '*in shā' Allāh*, next time'. That's what he said—'*in shā' Allāh*, next time'—and I wanted to slap him! This is what the *mushrik* would have said. This is what the people who didn't believe in Allah would have said. You're saying this?

The fact that I had my third daughter I can actually celebrate those words of the Prophet (*ṣallā Allāh ʿalayhi wa-sallam*) what bigger congratulations can there be? And yet we have done such a number in many cultures across the world on the stigma of having a daughter. Such a huge number has been done there are even mothers-in-law! Mothers-in-law are mad at their daughters-in-law because they didn't have a son. And they are yelling at them for not having a son! The kind of ignorance that is beyond imagination. You're a woman yourself! Do you realize what you are saying!? Do you realize how insane that is? She is putting her daughter-in-law down and threatening her, 'He's going to marry another one because you're not capable of giving him a boy'. The level of ignorance that we have reached and you would think these are people of Qur'an? These are people of *dīn*? And this ignorance, by the way, is not just limited to people who aren't religious. These are people with big beards and hijabs and memorizing Qur'an, *dīn* is everywhere else except here. What happened to these *āyāt*? Where did they go?

Ẓalla wajhuhū muswaddā—his face turns black, his face turns dark, he gets depressed and then Allah says he almost has no words—*min sū' mā bushshira bihī*—from the ugliness of the congratulations that he has been given. He's thinking why are you congratulating me? You should be feeling sorry for me. I wish you never told me and then Allah adds—*wa-huwa kaẓīm*—and he is constantly swallowing his anger.

وَإِذَا بُشِّرَ أَحَدُهُم بِٱلْأُنثَىٰ ظَلَّ وَجْهُهُۥ مُسْوَدًّا وَهُوَ كَظِيمٌ ﴿٥٨﴾

(النحل ١٦ : ٥٨)

When any of them is told about the birth of a female his face turns dark, and he is filled with suppressed anger.

(Al-Naḥl 16: 58)

He's not letting the words out. *Kaẓama* in Arabic to swallow anger. He looks like something bad tasting is in his mouth all the time. He hears the girl crying and it bothers him, it irks him. It's a humiliation to him. And on top of that:

> يَتَوَٰرَىٰ مِنَ ٱلْقَوْمِ مِن سُوٓءِ مَا بُشِّرَ بِهِۦٓ ۚ أَيُمْسِكُهُۥ عَلَىٰ هُونٍ أَمْ يَدُسُّهُۥ فِى ٱلتُّرَابِ ۗ أَلَا سَآءَ مَا يَحْكُمُونَ ﴿٥٩﴾
>
> (النحل ١٦ : ٥٩)
>
> and he hides himself from people because of the bad news, thinking: should he keep the child despite disgrace, or should he bury it in dust? How evil is their estimate of Allah!
>
> (Al-Naḥl 16: 59)

He stays away and covers himself up from meeting people. He doesn't like socializing with people because he is too embarrassed. They might ask him and he might even have to smile, have to say, 'Yeah, *mā shā' Allāh*, it's a girl'. He is saying *mā shā' Allāh* with a smile but inside he is dying. He is dying. And Allah is capturing this entire disgusting psychology, these disgusting emotions, Allah is painting all of them in these *āyāt*. *Yatawārā min al-qawm min sū' mā bushshira bihī*—he stays away from people, out of the ugliness of the congratulations he was given.

Ayumsikuhū ʿalā hūn—this was the *mushrik*'s thinking back in the day—should I keep holding on to this girl despite the humiliation. Should I just let her be even though this is such a terrible thing. You know the Arabs back in the day the worst thing they used to do is in the next words—*am yadussuhū fī al-turāb*—should he bury her in the dirt? That's what they used to do. Bury their girls alive. But then the more sane option, the more humane option for them was: I will let her stay alive but I am so angry at my wife, who gave birth to a girl, that I will put them in the tent next to mine. I will never speak to them again; I will leave the food outside; and I'll never go back there again. So these women are completely *muʿallaqah*—they are just left hanging. She can't go somewhere else and she is just sitting there because she had a daughter. That's her fault. These are his two options: should I stay with her even though it's humiliating or should I just bury this girl in the dirt and get the problem over with—*alā sā' mā yaḥkumūn*—what terrible decisions they make.

Now *al-ḥamd li-Llāh* we don't go that far, at least not to my knowledge. But you know Allah did not just highlight the crime of burying the child or abandoning the child, Allah highlighted everything from the facial expression onwards. This is something important to note in the Qur'an, Allah does not just criticize actions, Allah criticizes emotions. Allah criticizes facial expressions: *thumma naẓar, thumma ʿabasa wa-basar, thumma adbara wa-stakbar* (*al-Muddaththir* 74: 21-23). What is that? Somebody staring, frowning, just the facial expression is captured in the Qur'an as an expression of arrogance. In this case as an expression of *shirk*. As an expression of the lack of appreciation for what Allah has given you, so now, after these *āyāt*:

لِلَّذِينَ لَا يُؤْمِنُونَ بِٱلْـَٔاخِرَةِ مَثَلُ ٱلسَّوْءِ ۖ وَلِلَّهِ ٱلْمَثَلُ ٱلْأَعْلَىٰ ۚ وَهُوَ ٱلْعَزِيزُ ٱلْحَكِيمُ ﴿٦٠﴾

(النحل ١٦ : ٦٠)

> Those who do not believe in the Hereafter deserve to be characterized with evil attributes whereas Allah's are the most excellent attributes. He is the Most Mighty, the Most Wise.
>
> (Al-Naḥl 16: 60)

People who don't believe in the afterlife; they have the worst example, the example of the ugliest kind. Allah is saying this example—this scene that He has painted—is the epitome of ugliness. There is nothing uglier to Allah than this and this is a demonstration of people who have no expectations of standing in front of Allah. They have no *īmān* in the *ākhirah*. This disease! Can you imagine? How Allah makes something a big deal and we celebrate the exact opposite and don't see a problem with it. This is what happens when people abandon the Book of Allah.

So now He says: *wa-li-Llāh al-mathal al-aʿlā wa-huwa al-ʿAzīz al-Ḥakīm*—and for Allah is the highest example, going back to the *shirk* that they do, and He is the Ultimate Authority, All-Wise. And now, after He said this—Allah has said already these people are so bad, they don't even believe in the *ākhirah*—that should be enough, but He didn't stop there. Allah's anger at these kinds of people is so intense the next *āyah* is:

وَلَوْ يُؤَاخِذُ ٱللَّهُ ٱلنَّاسَ بِظُلْمِهِم مَّا تَرَكَ عَلَيْهَا مِن دَآبَّةٍ وَلَٰكِن يُؤَخِّرُهُمْ إِلَىٰٓ أَجَلٍ مُّسَمًّى فَإِذَا جَآءَ أَجَلُهُمْ لَا يَسْتَـْٔخِرُونَ سَاعَةً وَلَا يَسْتَقْدِمُونَ ﴿٦١﴾

(النحل ١٦ : ٦١)

> Were Allah to take people to task for their wrong-doing, He would not have spared even a single living creature on the face of the earth. But He grants them respite until an appointed term. And when that term arrives, they have no power to delay it by a single moment, nor to hasten it.
>
> (Al-Naḥl 16: 61)

If Allah were to grab people because of the wrong that they do, there would not be a single creature left alive on the earth. This crime, had Allah been one that will grab people as soon as they did a crime, the entire earth would have been wiped out as a result of this crime. *Wa-lākin yu'akhkhiruhum ilā ajal musammā*—however He gives them extra time, until a time that has been decreed by Him. *Fa-idhā jā'a ajaluhum, lā yasta'khirūn sāʿah wa-lā yastaqdimūn*—but when their time comes, when the deadline arrives, they're not going to be able to bring it any earlier and they're not going to be able to delay it any further.

Now we get to the *āyāt* that I started with:

وَيَجْعَلُونَ لِلَّهِ مَا يَكْرَهُونَ وَتَصِفُ أَلْسِنَتُهُمُ ٱلْكَذِبَ أَنَّ لَهُمُ
ٱلْحُسْنَىٰ ۖ لَا جَرَمَ أَنَّ لَهُمُ ٱلنَّارَ وَأَنَّهُم مُّفْرَطُونَ ﴿٦٢﴾
(النحل ١٦ : ٦٢)

They assign to Allah what they dislike for themselves and their tongues utter a sheer lie in stating that a happy state awaits them. Without doubt the Fire awaits them and it is to it that they shall be hastened.

(Al-Naḥl 16: 61)

They put for Allah what they hate themselves and their tongues make elaborate lies that they are going to have the best. No, no. Those people, they get the Fire. So many *āyāt*, one after the other after the other after the other about how angry Allah is at people who are saddened at the idea of daughters, they are saddened at that idea, *subḥān Allāh*!

Now let's think about the positive, let's switch the subject. What are we supposed to do with our daughters, what are they? When the Prophet (*ṣallā Allāh ʿalayhi wa-sallam*) says: *fa-aḥsana ilayhinna*; and in another hadith: *wa-ttaqā Allāh fīhinn*—he had *taqwā* of Allah when it came to them. When he spoke to them he had *taqwā* of Allah, when he thought about them he had *taqwā* of Allah, when he was thinking about getting them married he had *taqwā* of Allah. He wasn't thinking let me just get this over with, 'Why don't you just marry him? So what if you don't like him. Stop embarrassing my family. Just get married to your cousin,' and he forces her to get married. He has no *taqwā* of Allah.

A woman comes to *Rasūl Allāh* (*ṣallā Allāh ʿalayhi wa-sallam*) and says my father forced me to marry someone. What should I do? I didn't want to get married, but he still got me married. And he said that nikah is *bāṭil*, that marriage is null and void. It's cancelled; it doesn't count. How many Muslim girls are being forced into getting married, and when they say 'no' they get yelled at and psychologically tortured. 'Why are you not listening? Why are you making things hard on the family? What is wrong with you? Why are you embarrassing us like this? I knew I should have had a son.' They have to hear all this garbage. All this garbage.

All of it is done away with just one expression: *fa-aḥsana ilayhinna*, or *wa-ttaqā Allāh fīhinn*. The Prophet (*ṣallā Allāh ʿalayhi wa-sallam*) said when he talks to them, he has *taqwā* of Allah. They are going to be speaking on judgement day about what rights they had. Allah has given them certain rights and your job as *walī* is not to tell them what to do, but to protect their rights. That's your job as a father, that's my job as a father, to protect their rights. To ensure their happiness, not your happiness, their happiness. That's having *taqwā* of Allah in their matter. We tell them to have *taqwā* of Allah, so they should do whatever we want. It's the other way around.

This is the *amānah* of daughters: how softly we have to speak with our daughters, how kind we have to be with them. I've seen so many cases. There are people that email me from all over the world; the girl tells me my father tells me I'm fat and I'm ugly and nobody's going to marry me and I can't say anything because he's my father. So could you please tell me what to do? I don't know what to tell this girl. I do know what to tell her father though: *ittaqi-Llāh yā rajul*! How are you going to stand in front of Allah? Just because she lives under your roof, just because she was born in your family, just because she is under your *wilāyah*, does not mean you own her. She is the property of Allah; she is *amat-Allāh* just like you are *ʿabd-Allāh*. You will be standing in front of Allah; I will be standing in front of Allah, and we will have to answer for every word that comes out of our mouth.

Fa-aḥsana ilayhinna, wa-ttaqā Allāh fīhinn. He had to be good to them. Be your best to your daughters, show them your kindness, and show them your love. Instil confidence in them, believe in them. Ensure their happiness and then on top of that just any time you get even close to oppressing them, saying hurtful things to them just remember: *fa-aḥsana ilayhinna,* or *wa-ttaqā Allāh fīhinn*—you have to have *taqwā* in their matter.

I didn't even get into the words of the Prophet (*ṣallā Allāh ʿalayhi wa-sallam*): *wa-lam yu'thir waladahū ʿalayhā*—he doesn't prefer his sons over his daughters. You know what that means, right? My son gets older; I'm going to do all these things with him. No, you're going to do these things with him and your daughters. You're going to keep them with you. You're going to go on a trip? 'No, no, this trip is for the boys.' Yes, if there is a trip for the boys, then there better be another trip for the girls. Because if you want *jannah* that badly, you can't discriminate between the boys and the girls in your family. You as a father have to give equal love, this is our religion; it's beautiful. It's beautiful. We make life ugly for ourselves and for our children; we have to come back to the beauty that this religion is.

May Allah (*ʿazza wa-jall*) allow all of us to be good fathers, good brothers, and good *awliyā'* of our families.

May Allah (*ʿazza wa-jall*) never allow us to forget the obligation, the responsibility we have towards our daughters. The daughters that are reading this, don't email your father and say 'Abba read this'. Don't do that. Don't be selfish in your religion. You only want people to read what will make your life better. We started with this point. Everybody wants something for themselves and they give Allah the leftovers. People use religion to get their way. Allah knows when people use religion to get their way. This religion is not for you to use; this religion is for you to serve—to serve Allah; not yourself. Allah will protect you and Allah will protect your rights but don't use it as a weapon. Don't quote *aḥadīth* at people and *āyāt* at people.

In a sermon it's okay—that's my job. But inside the household, I'm not going to go and quote things to my wife or to my daughters and they shouldn't be quoting things at me. That's not what this *dīn* and its *āyāt* are for, not for arguments and winning arguments. That's abuse. Abuse of Allah's words, abuse of the words of the Prophet (*ṣallā Allāh ʿalayhi wa-sallam*), and so many people do it. A father is telling his daughter to do xyz and she doesn't want to do it. He says: *wa-bi-l-walidayn iḥsānā*—haven't you read Qur'an? That ain't about Qur'an, my friend. That's about what you want, and you are imposing it on her. Using the *āyāt* as a weapon, this is not right, that is not how it was *ever* done.

So may Allah (*ʿazza wa-jall*) protect us from being abusive to the word of Allah (*ʿazza wa-jall*) and the beautiful *Sunnah* of the Prophet (*ṣallā Allāh ʿalayhi wa-sallam*). May Allah (*ʿazza wa-jall*) soften our hearts towards our families especially our daughters. May Allah give us the ability to raise good daughters, good sons, that they may become the carriers of the future generations of Islam.

CHAPTER 9

Thoughts on Paris (Charlie Hebdo)*

In shā' Allāh, in this reminder, what I'd like to share with you are some reflections from the Qur'an, but inspired, really, by the tragic events that have taken place in France. These kinds of things, every time they come in the news, the Muslim mind almost freezes up; we get paralysed. How are we supposed to respond to this? We are barely done dealing with one tragedy, and another one hits in the news, and another one and another one. They are of different kinds: sometimes these are events in which some things are done to Muslims and other cases where Muslims have done some things to others; in both cases we are left completely baffled as to what an intelligent response is supposed to be or how we

* This reminder was given after the 7th January 2015 attack which took place in the offices of the French Satirical weekly newspaper Charlie Hebdo in Paris. Twelve people lost their lives in this attack.

are supposed to deal with this, not only as individuals but also as a community and in a larger sense as an ummah. I basically have four or five things to share with you here *in shā' Allāh*, and despite the frustration that you and I both feel about what is going on, I hope that I will be able to be coherent and consistent in the ideas that I want to present before you.

The first thing that I want to share with you is just a statement of fact: criminals are criminals. It doesn't matter what religion they have. When someone's a murderer and they murder someone who didn't deserve to be killed, it does not matter that they are Muslim or Jewish or Christian or atheist. They are equal before the law and they are equal before the eyes of Muslims. Just because someone commits a crime and they are a Muslim they are not any less guilty in my eyes or your eyes; that is not the case. Don't confuse the fact that: *innamā al-mu'minūn ikhwah*—all believers are brothers—that that should somehow confuse your sense of justice. Actually Allah (*ʿazza wa-jall*) in the Qur'an tells us very, very clearly to stand by justice: *wa-law ʿalā anfusikum*—even if standing by justice means you have to stand against your own selves. When Muslims have done something wrong, then it is something wrong; you cannot beat around the bush. The easy cop out for a lot of people when it comes to justice is, they confuse justice with retaliation.

What I mean by that is, and I'll give you a childish example so this point becomes clear, when one of your kids does something wrong and you tell them, 'You've done this wrong', and they say, 'Well, my brother did it. He did it too'. You know what? Anybody else doing something wrong does not justify your crime. You are responsible for your crime. And you cannot deflect and say, 'Well, what about them?' No, no, no. We'll deal with them separately. That's a separate problem; don't confuse their problem with what you have done. *ʿalaykum mā ḥummiltum*—you have to carry your own burden. Allah (*ʿazza wa-jall*) doesn't allow us to take credit for other people's work, and Allah (*ʿazza wa-jall*) doesn't allow us to justify our misbehaviour given other people's misbehaviour. He doesn't allow us to do that. *Lahā mā kasabat wa-lakum mā kasabtum*—they have what they earned and you have what you earned. That is the first point that I wanted to make.

The second is that these people are in fact an embarrassment. When Muslims—in the name of Islam—when they commit heinous acts then they are an embarrassment to the Muslim community but they are more than that. We are embarrassed and we are humiliated by what's happened, there's no way around it. Yes, I am not a criminal; I haven't done anything, but I do share something with them: these people are Muslim—or at least they claim to be—and apparently the things are done in the name of Islam. So long as that claim is there I have something in common with them, at least the word, and that enough is a humiliation. So now I want to address what does that mean for you and me?

First and foremost, we need to understand something. We have to take collective responsibility. That will be the last part that I discuss in my reminder. What does it mean to take collective responsibility? The ummah is in chaos and every single member—every single citizen of this ummah—his or her responsibility is to do something to undo that chaos. We have to do whatever we can in whatever capacity. Yes, we cannot get rid of chaos in the world, and we cannot get rid of fanaticism and craziness, we can't get rid of it; but we at least have the responsibility to do our part, at least our part. Know one thing for sure; one of the things that is spreading the chaos and helping further this craziness is that in the minds of some Muslims these people are actually somehow justified. Somehow what they did must be, in some sense, Islamic. And I want to just tell you unequivocally, without any confusion or any shadow of doubt—I've been trying to understand this *dīn* for well over a decade now and I have no doubts or no confusion in my mind—there's nothing Islamic about any of this. There is nothing even close to Islamic about any of this.

As a matter of fact, I personally give you the advice, I give my children the advice, and I give my friends the advice: don't watch those cartoons or those YouTube videos or those disparaging comments or read those books. I ask you not to read that stuff, I don't even want you to look at it because it's not worth your time. It's not worth it. But I will tell you one thing: as offensive as those cartoons may be it is equally offensive to do something in the Prophet's name, in Islam's name, in Allah's name (*subḥānahū wa-taʿālā*), that is against the teachings of Islam. It is equally offensive. When they are spreading filthy propaganda against Islam by insulting the religion; you're spreading another kind of propaganda against Islam by spreading hate and killing and injustice and calling that the *dīn* of Allah. That is also a crime, and we are equally offended by that too. That is a crime in itself.

This is the second point that I wanted to bring to your attention. They have no justification. Some people like to quote the example of Kaʿb ibn Ashraf, who was a famous poet at the time of the Prophet (*ṣallā Allāh ʿalayhi wa-sallam*), a Jewish Arab. He had extreme animosity towards the Prophet of Allah (*ṣallā Allāh ʿalayhi wa-sallam*). As a matter of fact, there are a number of occasions where he tried to corner Muslims and convince them to do exactly the opposite of what Allah would want them to do, or what the Messenger (*ṣallā Allāh ʿalayhi wa-sallam*) would want them to do; and *āyāt* came specifically about his conversations; on multiple occasions. This guy is so bad that his poison drew the attention of Allah (*ʿazza wa-jall*) and *āyāt* came responding to him, he's no ordinary enemy of Islam. Some people confuse his story because he was also a poet, and he made filthy poetry about Muslim women by name. Not just poetry against the Prophet (*ṣallā Allāh ʿalayhi wa-sallam*) which is bad enough, but on top of that the women of the Muslims. Now you and I imagine if somebody made dirty poetry about my daughter, about my sister, about my mother, how would I respond? And then some people confuse his story and say, 'Well it's because he made this poetry that the Prophet (*ṣallā Allāh ʿalayhi wa-sallam*) said: *man lī bi-Kaʿb*—"Who is going to get rid of Kaʿb for me"; and then a *Ṣaḥābī* got up and Kaʿb was finally killed, he was actually executed. It's because he made poetry, see, now we have justification'. You cannot just say whatever you want—this person made poetry and the Prophet (*ṣallā Allāh ʿalayhi wa-sallam*) commanded that he should be killed? Hold on a second!

This is the same man who actually attempted to kill the Messenger of Allah (*ṣallā Allāh ʿalayhi wa-sallam*) by poisoning his food—the idea of poisoning the food of the Prophet (*ṣallā Allāh ʿalayhi wa-sallam*) came from him. There are multiple occasions on which he made attempts to assassinate the Messenger of Allah (*ṣallā Allāh ʿalayhi wa-sallam*) including a secret conspiracy he had with Abū Sufyān, before he became Muslim, right after the loss of Badr. He went and had secret counsel with Abū Sufyān, among other instances. And, by the way, when he is living in Madinah and he is attempting to kill the Messenger (*ṣallā Allāh ʿalayhi wa-sallam*) by any means, then you know what that means? That means he attempted to assassinate the President. That is what you consider an enemy of the state and the penalty for that is death, in any state.

To take all of his career, and all of his animosity against the Messenger of Allah (*ṣallā Allāh ʿalayhi wa-sallam*), and to confuse that with: 'This guy made poetry, that's why we have to kill him'; and therefore anybody who says anything about Islam, anything about the Prophet (*ṣallā Allāh ʿalayhi wa-sallam*), anything about the Qur'an, we need to kill them. This is craziness.

This interestingly is an insight into how limited the thought process of the Muslim has become. Because the Qur'an and the legacy of all prophets is so huge but you want to take one story, which you don't even fully understand, and use that to decide whether you can take someone's life. The entire legacy of prophets is of them being made fun of—*ustuhzi'a rusul min qablik*—'messengers have been made fun of before you'. When Allah says they were made fun of that must not be a small joke, there must be some disgusting things beings said about messengers. Muslims have been made fun of before—*yasūmūnakum*—they would blacken your faces, the expression in Arabic suggesting the worst kinds of insults being hurled towards someone.

... وَلَتَسْمَعُنَّ مِنَ ٱلَّذِينَ أُوتُوا۟ ٱلْكِتَٰبَ مِن قَبْلِكُمْ وَمِنَ ٱلَّذِينَ أَشْرَكُوٓا۟ أَذًى كَثِيرًا ۚ وَإِن تَصْبِرُوا۟ وَتَتَّقُوا۟ ... ﴿١٨٦﴾

(آل عمران ٣: ١٨٦)

> ... you will certainly hear many hurtful things from those who were granted the Book before you, and from those who have associated others with Allah in His Divinity. If you remain patient and Godfearing ...
>
> (Āl ʿImrān 3: 186)

You're going to get to hear a lot of painful things from the People of the Book and the people that have done *shirk*. They're going to say some hurtful things towards you. By the way, that *āyah* in *Āl ʿImrān* is after the Battle of Uḥud; and you are going to hear horrible things coming from them—you're going to hear inciteful, hateful, ugly, disgusting speech coming from them. And what is Allah's response? What should you do? Kill anyone who speaks out?

No! *Wa-la-in taṣbirū wa-tattaqū*—if you could respond with *ṣabr* and you could have *taqwā*. So it's easy to ignore the entire Qur'an, the entire legacy of all prophets (*'alayhim al-salām*) including our own Messenger (*ṣallā Allāh 'alayhi wa-sallam*), who was insulted and cursed to his face on multiple occasions, with him not losing the smile on his face (*ṣallā Allāh 'alayhi wa-sallam*). Let's forget all of that, all of that is *munsūkh* (abrogated) because I want to kill someone. This is stupidity and it's an insult against Islam. I'm not addressing non-Muslims here, I'm only addressing Muslims—if you have the bug in your head that somehow what they did was Islamic, please get it out of your system and maybe spend some time learning the Book of Allah. Spend some time learning the *sīrah* of this Messenger (*ṣallā Allāh 'alayhi wa-sallam*) on whose behalf you speak. Because you clearly don't know who this man is, that you are standing to defend, and you don't know what it means to defend him (*ṣallā Allāh 'alayhi wa-sallam*). The first point was criminals are just criminals, no matter what. And even if they pretend to come up with religious justification, it changes nothing. It changes nothing. This is not a debate in Islamic studies. There is no argument to be had.

The third point that I want to make is that in fact hateful speech, condescending speech, insulting speech, speech made against our Prophet (*ṣallā Allāh 'alayhi wa-sallam*), cartoons made about him, or videos made about him, or things said about the Qur'an;

these things are offensive. And any people, any people including Muslims when they are insulted, when things that they hold sacred are insulted, they have a right to be offended. We have a right to be insulted that is part of our dignity. If it didn't hurt our feelings it would mean we have no dignity. That somebody could say something about my mother, someone can say something about my father, someone can say something about my Messenger (*ṣallā Allāh ʿalayhi wa-sallam*) and it doesn't affect me at all!? No, it affects me; it offends me; it angers me. I have a right to be angry but those are two separate issues. What's happening in the media now is these two are being made into one issue. In other words, we are against those people being killed unjustifiably and therefore we are for free speech; all of it should be celebrated. We are with them no matter what. No, no, no; for the Muslim it's not that simple.

These are two separate things; we are against people who are killed unjustifiably and we stand against those who killed them unjustifiably. Absolutely, there is no doubt about that, but at the same time we have a right and we will continue to have the right to be offended by that kind of ignorant and hateful speech; and we will speak out against it and we will stand against it. But there's a way to do it. We are not going to pretend that all free speech is lovely and we are supposed to be able to accept it. No; is Allah angered by the words of people, in the Qur'an? Absolutely. I just mentioned the *āyah* to you—the believers are going to be hurt by the words of other people. The issue isn't whether we have a right to be offended or not—we do—the issue is how do we respond? How do you react? And that reaction determines everything because our reaction to all things has to submit to the guidance of Allah and His Messenger (*ṣallā Allāh ʿalayhi wa-sallam*). It is not those feelings themselves; those feelings are justifiable, but what happens after those feelings that may not be justifiable. That's where the problem lies.

The final point that I want to bring to your attention in this reminder is actually something that I personally feel we don't talk about enough, and I think that's the real problem. That's the real point. The real point is why do people make fun of Islam? Why do they make fun of it anyway? Why do they insult it? Why are these cartoons being made? Why is there so much propaganda and so much hate speech towards Muslims, even justified as journalism nowadays, masked as editorial columns. The framing has become more and more interesting. It used to be radical Islam; so they talked about radical Islam and they talked about the Islam that these fanatics believed in; some crazy militant version of Islam where they just want to kill everyone, and they want to put women in garbage bags, and all this nonsense. But further down the line the definition of radical has loosened up to the point where, if you pray five times, now you're pretty radical. Radical used to be really crazy but now they are saying, if you even look too Muslim. If a woman is wearing a hijab she must be a radical Muslim; if a guy's got a beard he must be a radical Muslim. We don't have it that bad in the United States but in Europe it is pretty bad; and I've been to Europe and I can tell you it is pretty bad. It is seen as very radical, but the question is why?

We have this mentality, the Muslims have developed this mindset: 'They're out to get us man. These *kuffār*, they hate us. They keep making these cartoons against us, they keep doing this propaganda against us, they hate everything about Islam, they're coming after this, that and the other'. 'They', 'they', 'they'—we don't have any time to look in the mirror. The prophets (*ʿalayhim al-salām*) were also made fun of, as I told you. The *Ṣaḥābah* were also made fun of—*wa-yaskharūna min alladhīna amanū* (*al-Baqarah* 2: 212)—it's in the Qur'an: the *kuffār* made fun of those who believed. It's in the Qur'an, but the fundamental question is, why were they made fun of and why are we being made fun of? Is it the same thing? And I argue it is not. Those people were made fun of because that was one of the ways to shut down the work of Islam. One of the ways to stop Islam from spreading because they didn't know what else to do. Islam was so thought-provoking, Islam was so eye-opening, Islam called for justice, it questioned injustices happening in that society and people were gravitating—young people, old people—were gravitating towards Islam and they didn't know how to stop it. So they came out with the tactic of calling the Messenger (*ṣallā Allāh ʿalayhi wa-sallam*) a liar; and that didn't work. Maybe we can mock these people and just laugh them off so nobody thinks they are a big deal; that was one of their tactics; and when that didn't work they resorted to other tactics. All of these tactics were there to stop Islam from spreading because it was too powerful.

I don't argue that's the case with us. I argue Islam is being ridiculed because of how Muslims appear, what Muslims have become, how we carry ourselves, what our societies look like, what the streets look like in our neighbourhoods, what our homes look like, what our business practices are like, what our governments are like. If you want to look at examples of corruption, if you want to look at the exact opposite of a civilized society travel through the Muslim world—much of it. It's hard for us to even be civilized in the parking lot of a masjid for God's sake. The only time we are organized is when we have to be organized in *ṣufūf* (rows), when *ṣalāh* is called, but outside of that—forget about it! Just basic human decency, basic human decency we don't possess. We don't possess it.

What is Muslim civilization? We love quoting our history, we love quoting when the Muslims were at the forefront of invention; when they were leading the universities of the world; when people would come from all over the world to study *ʿilm* in Baghdad; when the Europeans had lost their literature and the Muslims had it and they had to come to us to learn it; when Spain was a model for the world. We love quoting those things, but what are you going to quote now? What have we done? What have we produced as a people? How have we contributed to the world? The only time we make it to the news is when we blow something up or we are in some kind of chaos or another. Look at it from the outside perspective: these people are crazy. These people are crazy. As a matter of fact I'm not even going to point the finger at the Muslim world—the rest of the ummah—let's think about Western Muslims for a moment.

We come to these societies, and I have dealt with the Muslim community in the United States for quite some time, and I have had decent interaction with the Muslim community in England and in Australia. But let me tell you something: the things you see among the Muslims—*subḥān Allāh*. I know Muslim business owners that lie on their taxes: 'Yeah, but I don't want to pay the *kāfir*'. Really? You don't want to pay the *kāfir*? You're selling beer. Your Islam didn't show up then but all of a sudden your—*walā'* and *barā'*—showed up when you had to pay your taxes. These Muslims! In fact not these Muslims, *we* Muslims! We have such low moral standards; such low moral standards. You have Muslim business owners that don't pay decent wages. They don't pay decent wages. They don't even give their wife her *mahr*. They are complaining about injustices in the world, they don't even have justice inside their home. Inside their home. Why would somebody want to be attracted to Islam?

The *āyah* that I want to share with you now is one of the scariest *āyāt* in the Qur'an when it comes to this ummah: *Rabbanā lā taj'alnā fitnatan li-lladhīna kafarū*—'Our *Rabb*, do not make us a *fitnah*, do not make us a tribulation for those who have disbelieved'. In other words one of the meanings of that *āyah* is, *yā Allāh* don't make us so wretched, so embarrassing a people, and so far from the actual beautiful teachings of Islam that when non-Muslims see us they say, 'Why would I want anything to do with Islam?' 'Why would I want to be Muslim?' 'Why would I want to be like these people?' 'This is what I want to be like?'

They are not justified in their poking fun but we are not justified when we refuse to look in the mirror. We have to start looking in the mirror. We have to fix this problem and it's high time we stopped complaining about what the world is doing against us. We are the people of *Lā ilāha illā Allāh*. We have on our side Allah (*ʿazza wa-jall*). His help is greater than any problem. There is no problem too big when you have Allah on your side. The problem is we don't want Allah's help, at least we don't care to earn it. It doesn't just show up for free, it has to be earned. There has to be a transformation that has to happen inside my house, it has to happen inside my family, it has to happen inside my neighbourhood. We have lost our moral compass and I am not talking about advanced knowledge of *dīn* and *fiqh* and Shariah, I'm talking about basic morality, people. Basic, basic morality.

We have *masājid* in the United States—and across the world even—where fund raising is taking place and they're going to collect money. Once they collect the money they are going to say, 'Yeah, we should put this money towards this thing or the other'. No, you advertised that you are going to raise these funds for this project but now you're putting it in another. 'No, it's okay, it's okay. We have a fatwa.' You have a fatwa to be dishonest? Where did you get that from? But that's okay for us, we can do that! We could lie even in the name of religion—*subḥān Allāh*! How can that be, how does it get to that point? How does it get to the point where you have to argue in your home, you have to argue with your parents, 'Dad, seriously, I really think we should give zakat'. 'No, no. It's okay';

and there is an argument happening inside a Muslim home whether they should give zakat or not. This is happening inside the Muslim family. Why would Allah's help come to a people like that; that have been given the most beautiful *dīn*, that have been given the most perfect teachings and they don't even look in the mirror for one minute, for one day just: 'What am I doing wrong?'

Many of you are not ulama, you're not *fuqahā'*, you're not muftis, you don't have to be. But you know what you do wrong, I know what I do wrong, and we keep overlooking it. Allah will not change the state of this people, Allah will not change the state of this ummah. Nope, He will not do it. Allah Himself says this. People say: 'Oh, you just quote the *āyāt*'. The *āyāt* are the ultimate reality. There is no greater reality than the *āyāt*. There is no reality you will find in physics and chemistry and biology that you won't find in the *āyāt* of the Qur'an. *Inna Allāh lā yughayyir mā bi-qawmin ḥattā yughayyirū mā bi-anfusihim*—Allah will not change the state of a people until they transform what is within their own selves (*al-Raʿd* 13: 11). *Mā bi-anfusihim*—there is something wrong inside of us, Allah's answer to what is wrong with the ummah is, something is wrong inside people. That is Allah's answer to what is wrong with this ummah today. When He says—*wa-antum al-aʿlawn in kuntum mu'minīn*—you are going to be in the supreme position, if in fact you have true *īmān*, if you are true believers (*Āl 'Imrān* 3: 139). Now, clearly we are not in the supreme position so something must be wrong with our *īmān* because Allah is never wrong. Allah is never wrong.

This is a tragedy. One after another, after another, after another; and it's not going to stop and we know it's not going to stop. The only thing we can do, instead of being overwhelmed by this flood of tragedy and constantly just figuring out a way to justify to people that we are not crazy, because, by the way, they are going to think we are crazy no matter what. You can't impress them, you can try, messengers tried too. If messengers weren't good enough for them, we're definitely not good enough for them, let me tell you. There is no way to impress them. No matter how we do right, the people who hate will always hate. The people who make fun will always make fun. But we better give them the right reasons to make fun of us.

The right reasons are we stand by Islam. We are the people of reason. We are the people of intelligence. The greatest threat of Islam was not its force, was not the sword, was not the weapon. The greatest threat of Islam was the power of its ideas; how it challenged injustice head on and how it questioned the integrity of other philosophies, other ideas. How can you think like that? How can you act like that? How can you judge like that? *A-fa-lā taʿqilūn*—why don't you think? How do you make your decisions? This is a religion of: *adʿū ilā Allāh ʿalā baṣīrah*—I call to Allah with eyes open—a religion of thought. We are no longer a thoughtful people, so Islam is no longer. We think, in the West, the threat of Islam is its militancy. The militancy is nothing—this is nothing. The real threat to the Quraysh—what rattled them—was not at Badr but back in Mecca. They were shaken up just by the *āyāt*, the word of Allah was enough. It was enough to take a tradition that was there for thousands of years and it was rattled just by a few words of Allah. Just by a few words. Something's happened, we are not connected with that word anymore.

You know, when somebody wants to win an argument, when two people have an argument and you don't have a response then you get angry, you start yelling. When you start yelling, it is proof that you've lost. When, in an argument, you start yelling, it is proof that you lost; because you don't have a reasonable answer left, and it frustrated you, so you got angry. When two people have an argument and you've lost and you hit the other, that is also proof that you lost; because you could not defeat him with words, so you figured you could try to defeat him with your hand. This is actually an indication that you're not strong enough in what you have to say.

My argument to you is that in our *dīn*, Allah has given us words—there are no stronger words, there is no stronger message. We don't have to resort to anything else and when we do, it is as though we are admitting that this isn't strong enough. But it is! *We're* not strong enough, because we are not connected to this word enough. We have to be the people that produce the most intellectual responses, the most reasonable responses, the ones that challenge the immorality of the world in the most profound and thought-provoking way. We're the ones that are supposed to engage in the deepest conversations with the agnostic, with the atheist, with the Christian, with all of them. Their accusation against religion, you know what it is? It's been there for centuries in Europe and now all over the world—religious people are closed minded, religious people are fanatical, religious people are intolerant, religious people cannot take criticism, religious people are not open to conversation—so if you get rid of religion you will have an open minded society where people can think for themselves.

This is their accusation and you know what? It holds true for the Christianity that had pervaded Europe for centuries; but the Islam that Allah gave His Messenger (*ṣallā Allāh ʿalayhi wa-sallam*) is the exact opposite of that. It is the religion that encourages dialogue—*hātū burhānakum in kuntum ṣādiqīn*—bring your evidence, why don't you give me all of your criticisms against the Qur'an, I would invite you to bring all of your criticisms. How is a book asking people not just to have faith but to please collect all of your criticisms and bring them. This is what you call open-mindedness, the book is calling to open-mindedness; we're the ones that are closed-minded; we're the ones. We have to empower this ummah again by opening up our minds, by opening up this book and thinking the way it wants us to think. To show that religion is not a way to close the mind, close the eyes and close the hearts. It is the way to open the mind, to engage in dialogue and to bring civilization to humanity. They think the solution is when you get rid of religion and we are saying the solution is when you bring the true religion. Yes, false religion will bring oppression; but when you bring the *dīn* of Allah, it's a thing of beauty.

If we don't show them that who will? That's why Allah put you and me on this earth, to be members of this ummah is an honour, it's not a small thing. We are carrying collectively—one-fifth of the world's population—on our shoulders, the burden that was placed on the shoulders of *Rasūl Allāh* (*ṣallā Allāh ʿalayhi wa-sallam*). That is what you and I carry every single day, whether we admit it or not. And when we don't do something about that burden, and we don't show humanity what it is, we're in trouble. Not just with the authorities, or with the media, we're in trouble with Allah.

I pray that Allah (*'azza wa-jall*) makes us a people of Qur'an once again. That we learn to think the way Allah wants us to think, and that we are able to represent in our character, in our communities, in our business dealings, in our personal lives, in our speech, in our demeanour we are able to depict what makes this *dīn* so perfect, what makes it so beautiful. May Allah (*'azza wa-jall*) shine the light of this guidance into all of our hearts, and keep it strong, and make it stronger and stronger; and may Allah make the generation of young people real leaders for this community who are going to bring an age of light out of this age of darkness.

CHAPTER 10

Naṣīḥah in Brief: The Dangers of Listening to Music

I don't have a bias against any particular culture or genre of music, but I have strong objections to music per se, though there is some scholarly discussion about it, but I will show you what I am convinced of. I think nowadays, listening to music of certain kinds is probably one of the easiest means to lose your moral sense. Some music is audio pornography, today. It's explicit, it's shameless, it's vulgar and it takes your sense of humanity away from you. It makes you look at women as objects—worse than objects—worse than animals, just assets. These people are talking about women like they are talking about an animal really. It objectifies women and especially I've noticed a lot of the brothers that I know of, Muslims, that are really into the hip-hop scene and they are kind of doing the *'ḥifẓ'* of the song. They are memorizing the song and they're really good at reciting it with perfect *'tajwīd'* too. And so they do that and it's just horrible language. Horrible, horrific, horrific language. The only simple response I have to that, if you have any regard for the Book of Allah, that you really think it's from Allah—*bi's al-ism al-fusūq baʿd al-īmān* (*al-Ḥujurāt* 49: 11)—even the name, the mention, the word for something bad, is terrible once you have faith. Even the mention of something terrible is horrible for you, is harmful for you, after you have faith. You have to have a clean tongue, you have to say what's best—*qul li-ʿibādī yaqūlū allatī hiya aḥsan* (*al-Isrā'* 17: 53)—tell my slaves to say that which is the best; say what is the best, say good things from your mouth.

This is the first thing, when you say horrible things and you say things that are in direct contradiction to the moral gauge Allah gifted us with then obviously you are deviating from your natural *fitrah*, your predisposition to turn to Allah. When you constantly listen to garbage like that then you get deviated and you don't find pleasure except in disobedience to Allah and that's the sign of a sick heart. So one has to distance themselves from this, this is the first step. And I'll tell you, this is my personal view; this is not a fatwa, it's my personal analysis, you don't have to take it, but if a person finds listening to the Qur'an annoying after they have been listening to hip hop, listening to it for a long time, and as soon as somebody puts the Qur'an on in the car you know what they say? 'Oh man, turn that off... I don't wanna...I just wanna talk.' Immediately, they get a little annoyed when they hear the Qur'an. That actually means the *shayāṭīn* have taken over and they are constantly making *waswasah* to this person; because what do the *shayāṭīn* hate the most? They hate the Qur'an, they hate the word of Allah. They flee from it. It hurts them. So you know what they do? Because this person has let the *shayāṭīn*, the devils, into his heart, they start pinching at his heart when he hears Qur'an, and he says, 'Ah, I don't want to hear this'. It's like pulling a tooth for this person. This happens when you try to give this person a reminder from Allah's word. They get annoyed by it—agitated—like an allergic reaction. Why? Because they have let the *shayāṭīn* in. To let them out the first thing you have to do is stop supplying them with fuel.

This is fuel. This useless wasting of time, this is fuel for *shayṭān*. They love that you waste your time. They love it because the one asset, the one piece of wealth Allah gave every human being, is time. And what is music, and TV, and YouTube, and Facebook, and Snapchat, and Twitter, and whatever else? If you're spending hours, and hours and hours on this stuff what is it except destroying your time? It's taking that one asset away from you; *shayṭān* will love nothing more. May Allah (*subḥānahū wa-taʿālā*) give you the strength to get away from these temptations. My advice that I keep repeating—I can't get enough of giving this advice—find better friends. Find company that is not into these things, and try to spend more time with them. *in shā' Allāh* you will wean yourself off these habits, *bi-idhni-Llāh*.

PART V

FOCUSING ON THE *ĀKHIRAH*

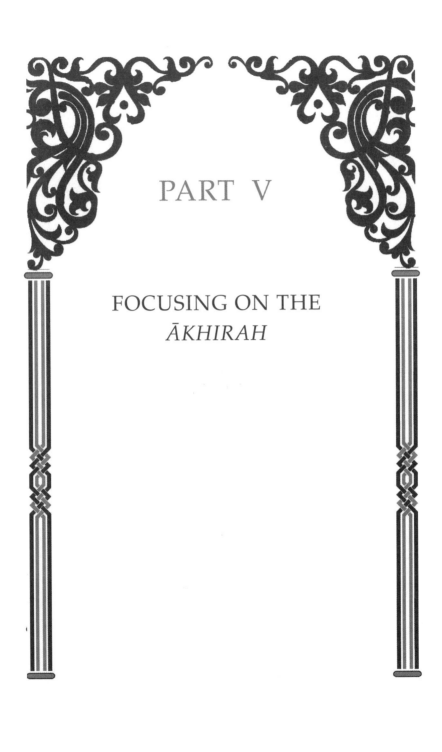

CHAPTER 11

Putting Life in Perspective

فَمَآ أُوتِيتُم مِّن شَىْءٍ فَمَتَـٰعُ ٱلْحَيَوٰةِ ٱلدُّنْيَا ۖ وَمَا عِندَ ٱللَّهِ خَيْرٌ وَأَبْقَىٰ لِلَّذِينَ ءَامَنُوا۟ وَعَلَىٰ رَبِّهِمْ يَتَوَكَّلُونَ ﴿٣٦﴾

(الشورى ٤٢ : ٣٦)

That which has been given to you is only the wherewithal of the transient life of this world. But that which is with Allah is better and more enduring for those who believe and put their trust in their Lord.

(Al-Shūrā 42: 36)

It was very difficult for me to choose an *āyah* for this reminder and I've been thinking about it for some time. I realized at the end of all that thinking that our religion, by definition, is simple and its teachings are straightforward. So I don't have to make something complicated when, by definition, it's supposed to be simple. This reminder is a reminder that I need, that I think everyone in this room needs and it is something that we constantly have to live with. It's so easy to remind ourselves of but, at the same time, it's very, very easy to forget. I want to start with just a rough translation of the *āyah* that I recited before you.

Allah (*'azza wa-jall*) in *Sūrat al-Shūrā*, the forty-second surah, says: *Fa-mā ūtītum min shay'in fa-matā' al-ḥayāt al-dunyā*. 'Then whatever you've been given'—*fa-mā ūtītum*, and the word *mā* suggests that there's an openness: anything that you've been given. And in addition to all of that, it's *min shay'in*. You could say *mā ūtītumūhu*—it could have been a pronoun; but instead of adding a pronoun, it's *min shay'in*, and not even *shay'an*; it's *shay'in*, which is very unusual language. It suggests any and all things, that you can imagine, that you have been given. Now in using those two words together, in the *āyah*, Allah is talking about every single object, physical object that you own whether it's clothing, a car, a house or whatever you own, down to a pen that's to your name. In addition, Allah is also talking about whatever you and I have been given in terms of life experiences. What kind of parents we have been given, what kind of youth, what kind of opportunities we were given, what kind of friends you and I were given? Everything that I have been given, everything that I have experienced in my life thus far is inside, *fa-mā ūtītum min shay'in*. It's captured within it.

So this *āyah* is going to make a commentary about my entire existence on this earth. Before I go any further, a reflection just on the fact that the passive form was used, *ūtītum*—that you've been given. In other words, none of the experiences I've enjoyed—not just the things that I own or that I think I own—rather none of the experiences that I had in life are actually mine. They were a door that was opened to me by Allah (*subḥānahu wa-taʿālā*). He was the one that opened every chapter of my life, one adventure to the next, to the next, to the next. For those of you that are married; who you married, and if there was a process before you got married, every part of that process was actually from Allah. Every single conversation was from Allah. This entire story of ours—and we don't remember so much of it. When we look back we don't remember so many things that happened in our own lives, but they were all from Allah.

Actually, the last ten years, it's becoming more and more of a blur for me. I don't know what I was up to in 2007, I can't tell you, I don't know. It's just becoming blurred together; I can't tell you what happened in 2011 or 2012. I look at my children and they're growing. My now almost twelve year old, I look at her and it's hard for me to remember what she looked like when she was four. I have to look at a picture to try and remember, I can't remember that anymore. But Allah (*ʿazza wa-jall*) gave me each and every one of those experiences—whether I remember them, or I am conscious of them or not. All of them together, Allah sums up in one phrase *fa-matāʿ al-ḥayāt al-dunyā*. Basically, the culmination of all of our life experience, whatever good, whatever bad, or whatever we think was good or bad happened to us, boils down to one thing: *fa-matāʿ al-ḥayāt al-dunyā*—which is roughly translated as: the enjoyment of worldly life. All the things that you have been given; all they are is just the enjoyment of worldly life.

I wanted to explore, in this reminder, the meanings of the word *matāʿ* in a little more depth. More than what we've heard before. Those of you that have been listening to my *khuṭab* and *durūs* before, I've discussed *matāʿ* before as something to utilize but not necessarily to enjoy. This is part of the base meaning like that little girl, who al-Aṣmaʿī saw, who was scrubbing dishes at the bank of a river. Her goat came, grabbed the scrubber and ran away with it. She started crying and saying, *akhadha matāʿī*—he took my *matāʿ* away—the brush that I was scrubbing with, right? So from it he derived that *matāʿ* must amount to things like a spoon, or a fork or a shovel something that you use but you don't necessarily enjoy. Nobody grabs a spoon and says, 'Check this out! Check what I've got!' Nobody shows off their spoons and forks and shovels unless they're in the industry or something, but typically, you don't do that. So it's something that you use but you don't necessarily enjoy. But I decided to dig a little bit deeper into this word and see what else has been said in the literary precedent of the Arabic language because at the end of the day this word, like this *āyah*, has pretty significant importance. My entire life is being summed up by this one word. My whole life, on this planet, amounts to this one word. So I should understand what connotations this word possesses.

The first thing I found interestingly—very recently actually—they used *mataʿa al-nabīdh* for wine. This is pre-Islam obviously, *mataʿa al-nabīdh: ishtaddat ḥumratuhū*—when the wine gets redder and redder, it matures. When it reaches the point that it possibly can't mature any more—it has reached its climax—that's when they say it has reached the state of *matāʿ*. In other words, when something reaches as far as it can go, when something reaches maturity.

Let's go a little further, the Arab say: *ḥablun mātiʿ*—which is actually used for a rope that is twisted and coiled well together. Something that is twined well, not only does it have this idea of being twined, but also the idea that the rope is now ready for use. Because when you twine a rope properly; it's matured. No more work needs to be done on it. Now it can be put to use. They use it for people: *mataʿa* or *matuʿa al-rajul*—when a person, becomes mature and becomes refined in his character, meaning he can now go out and deal with the world. He can go do business now—he's graduated from certain pre-requisites. He is ready to be used. That's the idea of a human being reaching *matāʿ*.

Then, *al-māti*ʿ *min kulli shay'*—at the end of the day, this is the most comprehensive definition I have found and I want to finish these definitions before I share some thoughts with you about this *āyah*. *Al-mātiʿ min kulli shay': al-bāligh fī al-jawdah*—that anything that reaches *matāʿ*, anything that becomes *mātiʿ*—that's the *ism fāʿil* (active participle) form—anything that becomes this, is actually something that has reached the most maturity it possibly can. *Al-ghāyah fī bābihi*—the most possible within it. *Fa-amma al-matāʿ fī-l-aṣl: kullu shayin yuntafaʿu bihi*— *matāʿ* is actually something that can be benefitted from. Let's stop there for a second—we'll stop at every piece of this definition. First it was mature, it can't mature any more. So, Allah is saying whatever experiences happened to you, part of the reason for giving you these experiences is they're going to mature you. This is part of you growing. The good things and the bad things that happen to you and me are part of us growing. Part of our growth is sometimes things that we are proud of and sometimes they are things that we're not proud of. Things that we've done, we look back and we say, 'I'm glad we've done those things' and there are things we look back and we say, 'I wish

I never did those things'. Well actually that was part of your *matāʿ*; it was part of your growth and maturation process. Even the regret that you feel looking back, that regret is a gift from Allah. That regret alone might save you. That might be the reason for you and me to enter *jannah*. I'm reminded, in *Sūrat al-Kahf*, of the gardener who, at the end of his tragic experience of losing his beautiful garden says, *yā laytanī lam ushrik bi-rabbī aḥadā*—he has regret, 'I wish I never commit *shirk*! Look at what's happened to me?' But actually that regret is a happy ending to that story because at least now he's turned back to Allah. He's changed his ways. So the first thing is that everything in life is there to mature you.

The second thing: *mā yuntafaʿu bihi*—what can be benefitted from. Think about this definition of *matāʿ*; every experience in life is something you can benefit from. Allah chose this word for a reason. There was some good in it for you even though you may not be able to see it. You may not be able to recognize it at face value and it may be frustrating at that very moment. It may be something where your first response would be, 'Why would this be happening to me?' And Allah's way of responding to us is that Allah is saying that it's something you could have benefitted from—*yuntafaʿu bihi*.

Then: *wa-yutaballagh wa-yutazawwad*—and it can be put to use. It can be put to use—*yutazawwad bihi*. Now

Allah is saying every single object that we own, every last bit of our possessions and every single experience is actually supposed to be utilized. Adversity and good times, all together, are supposed to be put to use. They are part of something greater. Meaning this life, the things that we are given, they are given to be put to use.

This takes us back to the original meaning of *matāʿ*. What happens to wine? Not by Muslims but by non-Muslims, what happens to wine or to alcohol, when it matures? It gets drunk. What happens to the rope when it gets twisted? It gets used. When your life is full of *matāʿ*, now it's time for you, yourself, to put yourself to use. Looking back, for a lot of people when they look back at their life, their past experiences, their failures and their tragedies; they debilitate them and they are not able to do anything in their future. But for people who understand what *matāʿ* is, what this world is for, they look at their past experiences and it makes them stronger. That Allah put me through that must mean I'm stronger than this and maybe I can help a million other people; help them go through these experiences and see them in the way that they're supposed to be seen. This would be looking at one's own experiences as *matāʿ*.

Now going a little further—*wa-l-fanā' ya'tī ʿalayhi*—part of the definition of *matāʿ* is something that will come to end; will not last. It cannot be used forever. That scrubber will break eventually, or won't scrub as good as it used to. That rope will eventually snap. Even that wine will eventually be no good. So, every single thing that we possess is not here forever.

Today we are a senior living, in a facility where people that have a difficult time taking care of themselves are being taken care of. And where I teach at Bayyinah, the average age among our students and the faculty that's there, it's younger people. There's typically a young audience in the Jumuʿah. We feel like we have some things that they don't have. Someone might feel, as they walk by someone who's in their nineties, or someone who's using a cane, or someone who can't even take two steps by themselves—they might look at them and say, '*Subḥān Allāh,* I feel bad for these people'. But you know what? Either we're going to be in the ground or we're going to be one of those people; we're going to be in that state one day. And they, if you ask them, 'Look back at what you had in life', they'll say, 'It felt like a day or like the blink of an eye—*lamḥ al-baṣar*—that's all it felt like'. Time passes by so, so quickly, *subḥān Allāh.* We have to be conscious of the fact that time is leaving us. This *matāʿ* is not staying. Our entire life is passing us by and the only thing, at the end of it, that we can put it to use for is the *ākhirah*.

So Allah says: *wa-mā ʿind Allāh khayrun wa-abqā*. What I want to share with you is that in this life, sometimes we make a plan for the next ten years or five years. This is what I want to accomplish; this is how much Qur'an I want to memorize; this is how much I'd like to be able to make in terms of money; this is when I would like to get married. We set goals for ourselves and we strive towards those goals, and there's nothing wrong with that. But I tell you if you internalize this *āyah*. You learn to put those plans in one compartment in your head, and in the other compartment you realize that all of that means nothing if I'm not building my *ākhirah*. All of those plans are worthless; they are meaningless; they are not any kind of accomplishment at all, if this is not building me towards Allah, if it's not taking me closer to Him, if it's not making me a slave of Allah.

There are people's perceptions of us and then there's the reality. People's perception, our own perception and the reality. People's perceptions may be you're successful; people's perception may be your knowledgeable or you've accomplished something. And the opposite is true too, people's perception might be, you're worth nothing but you know what? People's perceptions, at the end of the day, mean nothing. It stands to give you nothing before Allah. It will not add to your deeds, it won't take away from them. People's criticisms will not take away from you and people's praise will not add to you. It will not. At the end of the day, when people get praise and criticism from others all the time, you know what starts happening? They start getting affected by it. They start seeing themselves in light of how other people see them. So their image of themselves becomes polluted because they're not seeing themselves for who they really are, they're seeing themselves in light of other people's words. That's a human phenomenon. This is why we have Allah's word. So we can see ourselves in light of Allah's words; and that will help us see ourselves for who we really, truly are.

At the end of the day, truly, we can have friendships and family and loved ones and community, we can have all of those things. But at the end of the day, we are in this world alone. We came alone, and we are going to leave alone. And in that solitude, if you don't find a connection with Allah, then all these fake connections that you and I have, that are not really based on a relationship with Allah, they will all disappear. They will not last. The façade will dissipate eventually, if not in this life then in the next. So we have to internalize a very powerful reality that Allah has given us: *fa-mā ūtītum min shay'in fa-matāʿ al-ḥayāt al-dunyā*. We treasure all of our relationships so long as, they are something that is building us towards the *ākhirah*.

So I want to leave you with this picture: *wa-mā ʿind Allāh khayrun wa-abqā*—what Allah has in His possession is better. What we have right now is also in Allah's possession—it's not like this is not in the possession of Allah. But by using the word *mā* here it is as though Allah is saying, 'I don't want to tell you what I have yet'. I have a mystery for you. There is something I have in my possession and it's better, it's better. In other words it hasn't been given to you yet. Now, one would immediately think what Allah has? He must be talking about *jannah*. But as a matter of fact because he opened the door by saying *mā ʿind Allāh*—not *wa-l-jannatu khayrun wa-abqā*. He said, *mā ʿind Allāh khayrun wa-abqā*—whatever Allah has. And what Allah has, some of which he gave to you now, not just in terms of *dunyā* but He also gave you in terms of that road to *jannah*. That road itself is better. The revelation of Allah is better than everything else you've been given. The word of Allah is better because, if you and I can live by it, it'll get us somewhere far better.

So in this *āyah* there are two comparisons that we constantly have to make, if we are going to survive this world and not be taken in by the perceptions that are actually not real—the perceptions of people or the false self-image that we might develop. What is that reality check?

... وَمَا عِندَ ٱللَّهِ خَيْرٌ وَأَبْقَىٰ لِلَّذِينَ ءَامَنُوا ... ﴿٣٦﴾
(الشورى ٤٢ : ٣٦)

... But that which is with Allah is better and more enduring for those who believe ...

(Al-Shūrā 42: 36)

Whatever Allah has is firstly, better and secondly, lasts longer—as far as those who really have *īmān* are concerned. So now every experience in life I compare to something else that Allah has, and what Allah has must be better. It's a small reminder; you go into the store to buy yourself some new clothes. The moment you're putting those on the cash register, just at that moment, think—*wa-mā ʿind Allāh khayrun wa-abqā li-lladhīn āmanū*—what Allah has, the clothing Allah will give me is better. Whatever is acceptable with Allah in *jannah* for me is better, for those who believe. We're about to eat some good food, you enjoy the food, if you could tell yourself right as you're eating—*wa-mā ʿind Allāh khayrun wa-abqā li-lladhīn āmanū*—the *ākhirah* doesn't just become some clichéd thing you bring up; or you only bring up when somebody's going through trouble. 'No, No, *in shā' Allāh*! Allah will give you in the *ākhirah*.' It becomes a part of your daily life. The *ākhirah* becomes something you think about all the time. Because Allah didn't just describe it as something that is there in the heavens, He described it as something that is with Allah. Now what does *ʿinda* mean? *ʿInda* suggests closeness, so the acquisition of *jannah*, necessarily means closeness to Allah. So what Allah is offering, in this *āyah* also, is closeness to Him—*wa-ʿalā Rabbihim yatawakkalūn*—they place their trust in Allah. I tell you, if you and I develop this attitude, then worldly possessions and worldly gain and worldly loss will become easy to deal with.

Relationships become easy because if you realize, what Allah has is better, the next time you get into a quarrel—some kind of tension between you and a friend, you and a family member and your pride gets in the way of fixing those tensions. We must realize that what Allah has is better, and this world is going to go before we know it. Before we know it this will mean nothing. There are people that have ruined relationships for years because their pride gets in the way of apologizing. They can't get themselves to say sorry. 'No, I'm not going to say sorry; it's the other one's fault. Why should I say sorry?' And they're going to take that to their grave. They didn't have much time here and, by the way, when we're standing in front of Allah, the pride's going to be gone. You and your brother, that you were angry with, are both standing in front of Allah and you're both begging Allah for mercy. Had you forgiven each other you could have both earned *jannah*. Just by the act of forgiveness. When you put it in perspective, is your pride really worth that much? Is your anger really that heavy that you couldn't earn yourself what Allah is offering?

When things are put in this perspective, life becomes easy to deal with. We learn the expression: *kabbirhā takbur ṣaghghirhā taṣghur*—make something big and it becomes a big deal; make something small, it becomes a small thing. Well you know what? This *āyah* is about making *ākhirah* big and making *dunyā* small. That's all it's about! We're going to go through life, we're going to have careers, we're going to have educational accomplishments, we're going to have challenges, all of those things are going to be there. But, you know what? These are all temporary. These are all temporary.

One day will come, there will be a congregation, they're going to make *ṣalāh* and they're going to make an announcement that there's a *janāzah* and it's going to be mine; and it's going to be yours. It's going to happen. People are going to pray over us and then we're going to be gone. And it's sooner rather than later, I mean quite a bit of our life has already passed us by. So it's not like we are getting further away from that day, we're only getting closer. So the sooner we internalize that, whatever Allah has is better—because we're heading towards it anyway—we're just doing ourselves a favour. If we could just learn to utilize our time in the right way. We make ten-year plans and fifteen-year plans, yet we don't think about the *ākhirah*.

Then, how do you think about the *ākhirah*? How do you practically plan for the *ākhirah*? You don't make a ten-year plan, you don't make a fifteen-year plan for the *ākhirah*—you make a daily plan. It's not about making long term goals; it's about how did you spend today? What are you going to do after Jumuʿah? How are you going to spend tomorrow? When are you going to wake up? What are you going to do with your free time? When are you going to erase those useless games off your phone? When are you going to stop watching so much TV? When are you going to stop? When are you going to stop wasting time just chatting away or trolling? When are you going to stop? When are you, going to hold yourself, to a higher standard, if not today? If you don't make that change in your day—how you go to sleep, how you wake up, what you say and what you do, especially how you spend, what you think is, free time? Because it's not free—you're not paying for it now but you and I will be paying for it with Allah. We will be paying for it. There is a price. We may not realize we're going to be paying for it, but it's on record.

You know how people feel relaxed when they are off the clock, when they punch out of the office. Well we're constantly on the clock with these angels. They don't take a break, and when they do they put the alternatives on shift. So that plan has to be made for our day; and *in shāʾ Allāh taʿālā,* Friday is a great day to start new habits. Friday is a great day for introspection. We take extra time out for *ʿibādah* anyway; we take extra time out to get ready to meet Allah anyway on this day. Allah already enables us to become spiritually more powerful, more strengthened, this day than other days. So why not make some serious commitments to yourself? This is not for you to share with anyone else—this is just you and yourself. You are, your worst critic, when it comes to this. You and I have to decide how we are going to live our lives differently because, *wa-Llāhi* the moment we start saying, 'I'm doing pretty good', that 'actually I have nothing to change in my life, I'm set'—that delusion, it must be that so many other people have given us that false sense of delusion. They've blinded us for so long; they've poured so much dust in our eyes that now we can't even see who we are for ourselves.

I pray that Allah (*ʿazza wa-jall*) does not make us of those that are blinded to their own reality. I pray that Allah (*ʿazza wa-jall*) constantly makes the Book of Allah a mirror through which we can see the truth of who we are and constantly seek to improve ourselves.

CHAPTER 12

Small Beginnings

In a *khuṭbah* I once gave on *Sūrat al-Kahf*, I talked about the parable Allah gave of two gardeners that have a conversation with each other. In this reminder, I'd like to share with you the conversation right after that lesson that Allah taught us. There also Allah says—*wa-ḍrib lahum mathal al-rajulayn*—We strike for them the example of two men. Here again He says—*wa-ḍrib lahum*—strike an example for them. This command to strike an example seems strange in English. I'll reflect on this a little bit with you. This is actually a command given to our Prophet (*ṣallā Allāh 'alayhi wa-sallam*). The Qur'an is Allah's address to humanity—Allah is talking to all human beings. But in these kinds of instances instead of telling us directly and saying—*naḍrib lakum al-amthāl*—We're going to give you an example; instead Allah commands His Prophet (*ṣallā Allāh 'alayhi wa-sallam*) to talk to the people. Why is that? Because Allah

(*ʿazza wa-jall*) in these *āyāt* highlights the importance of the Messenger (*ṣallā Allāh ʿalayhi wa-sallam*).

The Qur'an cannot be understood without the best teacher whom Allah (*ʿazza wa-jall*) appointed to teach this Qur'an. You can think of the Qur'an like the curriculum but a curriculum is only as good as the teacher who teaches it. So at the end of the day, even though the lessons are from Allah (*ʿazza wa-jall*), Allah appointed the best teacher in humanity to teach those lessons and that is the Messenger himself. So the *āyah* itself is very powerful but the *āyah* will not carry its impact until the Messenger (*ṣallā Allāh ʿalayhi wa-sallam*) teaches it to the *Ṣaḥābah* (*raḍiya Allāh ʿanhum*). So Allah is saying: 'You give the example to them, when you give them the example it will have a different effect'. From this not only do we learn the importance of the Prophet (*ṣallā Allāh ʿalayhi wa-sallam*) himself, as a teacher of the Qur'an, we also learn a *Sunnah* of Allah (*ʿazza wa-jall*); and that is that the Qur'an and its lessons have to be shared by a teacher to students—that it's not just a personal experience but it's a communal experience.

We have to actually talk about the Qur'an to each other, the *amr* is: *khāṣṣatan li-l-nabī wa-lākin iḍāfatan lanā kadhālik*—the command is specifically to the Prophet (*ṣallā Allāh ʿalayhi wa-sallam*) and that is *khāṣṣ* for him, especially for him, but it extends to all of us also; all the believers. We have to actually engage in reminding each other from the Qur'an, and it has an effect when a believer reminds another believer from the Qur'an. It's a different effect from when you read the Qur'an by yourself and when you read *tafsīr* by yourself, it's a different effect. There's something about human communication and *naṣīḥah,* Allah put something special in it. And so the command in the beginning is give them the example, strike an example for them. Not even saying: *aʿṭihim mithāl*—give them an example. Rather, He says: *wa-ḍrib lahum mathalan*. What does that mean? *Ḍaraba* in Arabic means 'to strike', and this figure of speech is used in Arabic when you say something that is going to have an impact.

You know when something hits something; it causes a noise, it creates a disruption and everybody's attention goes that way. If you're sitting in your office, quietly working and you hear a crash outside. You're going to look out the window promptly because something hit something else and immediately the noise gets your attention. You're going to sleep at home and you hear something fall in the kitchen; immediately you think what's going on over there? Let me go and check what's happening. The striking of something is actually a cause of attention—*khudh al-intibāh minhum*—take their attention; grab their attention when you give the example. What Allah is teaching us is that there are opportunities when we can get each other's attention. There are other times when you can talk to somebody and give them an example or try to give them *naṣīḥah* and advice, but their attention is somewhere else, that's not the right time to give them advice.

A lot of times I'll go to a nikah, or a *walīmah*, or something like that; and people are enjoying each other's company, they are eating food, kids are running around, and they say: 'Brother, give a talk'. People are eating, they are talking to each other, somebody's on the cell phone. This is not the time. This is not the time, because they are not going to pay attention. The kids are screaming in the back, there are people that are already engaged in their own conversation; you have to find the right time to give the advice, the right time and right setting to give the advice. I'm not saying that setting has to be the masjid alone, but you have to be intelligent enough to know when is a good time to talk about something that will actually carry impact. You're trying to give a brother advice and he's on the phone. That's probably not a good time. Let him finish his conversation; let him not be busy with something else when you talk to him. Even that is embedded inside *wa-ḍrib lahum*.

وَٱضْرِبْ لَهُم مَّثَلَ ٱلْحَيَوٰةِ ٱلدُّنْيَا كَمَآءٍ أَنزَلْنَٰهُ مِنَ ٱلسَّمَآءِ فَٱخْتَلَطَ
بِهِۦ نَبَاتُ ٱلْأَرْضِ فَأَصْبَحَ هَشِيمًا تَذْرُوهُ ٱلرِّيَٰحُ ۗ وَكَانَ ٱللَّهُ عَلَىٰ كُلِّ
شَىْءٍ مُّقْتَدِرًا ﴿٤٥﴾

(الكهف ١٨ : ٤٥)

> (O Prophet), propound to them the parable of the present life: it is like the vegetation of the earth which flourished luxuriantly when it mingled with the water that We sent down from the sky, but after that the same vegetation turned into stubble which the winds blew about. Allah alone has the power over all things.
>
> (Al-Kahf 18: 45)

And what does Allah do at the end of this example of the two gardeners? He says: *mathal al-ḥayāt al-dunyā* let me give you an example of worldly life altogether; all worldly life. The word *al-ḥayāt* itself—'life'—when you say life to anybody, for example, when you say to a non-muslim, 'How's life, man?' He's not going to think life in the hereafter. When you say, 'How's life?', what they are thinking of is this life—how is your life right now? Every human being understands when you say *al-ḥayāt*, it means life right now. But Allah says: *al-ḥayāt al-dunyā*—He adds the word *al-dunyā*, and some ulama, like Ibn ʿĀshūr, comment: *fīhi maʿānī al-ḥaqārah*—it actually includes the meanings of putting something down. Allah says give them the example of the lowest form of life. *Dunyā* actually comes from *adnā*—it's the feminine form of *adnā*, and the verb *danā* is something that's closer or something that's lower. *Al-dunyā* is the superlative form, the most extreme form. So what that means is: 'Give them the example of the lowest possible life'.

You see human beings were created for *jannah.* Our first residence was *jannah* and we were brought to this place. We were brought to this earth and even though Allah's earth is full of blessings for us, as Allah himself teaches us, our life is actually meant for something much higher. As great as this world is, it's still the lowest form of life—*al-dunyā.* This is the minimal level. Give them the example of this life that they get so caught up in. So what example does Allah decide to give us in this beautiful *āyah*? He says: *wa-ḍrib lahum mathal al-ḥayāt al-dunyā ka-mā'*—and before I discuss this parable it's important to know that the word *mathal* is different from *mithl.* Sometimes Allah uses *mithl,* sometimes He uses *mathal. Mathal* is used when every part of the example Allah will share has a lesson in it. *Mathal* is multi-dimensional. There are multiple things to learn in a *mathal.* In *mithl,* there is only one comparison: *huwa mithluhu*—he's like him. That's it. It's a one to one analysis but in a *mathal,* it's a multi-dimensional thing. You have to look at it and pay attention to every little detail.

So Allah begins describing your life and mine. First, He tells us that this life is the lowest one—don't get so caught up in it. The benefit of that is we don't get too attached to this *dunyā.* The joys of this world and the tragedies of this world are difficult. The tragedies are difficult to deal with; the joys are not. It's not easy for you not to get overworked about them, but if you can keep in mind that this is temporary and something much bigger is ahead, then this problem becomes a small problem. Just to give you an example of what I am talking about before I go into Allah's example: if you and your brother have an argument—you have a fight with each other—and you are blood brothers, siblings. You live next door to each other but you got into a fight, now you don't talk to each other. It's been a couple of months and you haven't talked to each other.

But one day you wake up, and your house is on fire, you can smell the smoke; and obviously your houses are attached. So if your house is on fire, what's the danger? His house is on fire too. What are you going to do? Are you going to say: 'I'm not going to tell him, I haven't talked to him in three months it's going to be awkward if I knock on his door and say, "Hey bro, I know we haven't talked but the house is on fire." Nah, forget them'. No! There is a bigger problem, when there is a bigger problem you forget the smaller problem. It's no longer a problem, 'Come on, let's go! Let's go!' So what happens? When there is a bigger thing ahead, there's a bigger danger ahead, then all your problems disappear, because you have to deal with the bigger thing. Our understanding of the *ākhirah* is just like that. We have issues with each other, but when we realize that there is a bigger danger you and I have to face—it's *yawm al-qiyāmah*—when you keep that in mind, then our problems become small. Our problems are easy to resolve because there is a bigger more prioritized thing ahead of us that we have to worry about.

So now Allah says: *ka-mā'*—the example of worldly life is like water. He doesn't even say: *al-mā'*—He says *mā'* in the indefinite—which here actually means 'a little bit of water'. And water as we know is the ultimate form of *rizq* in this world. All of us survive because of water. Vegetation on this earth is a product of water. You and I have to have a daily intake of water. Life is a function of water. So, the ultimate wealth on this earth is water, and because we are in an intensely capitalistic world now there are people that understand the scarcity and power of water and they are actually buying up water resources all over the world. In history, water has been a public resource, water has never been a property owned by an individual. But now there are companies out there that are literally buying out reservoirs of water, because they understand, in a few years to come, because of all the pollution human beings have caused on the earth, water itself will become the next oil. Water itself will be the next major resource. So companies like Coca Cola are actually buying out lakes and rivers and properties from governments all over the third world—it's crazy. So, perhaps in the future we will realize what kind of treasure water itself is. But in this *āyah* Allah says a little bit of water and a parallel to that is; a little bit of money, a little bit of this, a little bit of something. *Anzalnāhu min al-samā'*—immediately He mentions even if it is a little bit, He sent it down from the sky. A little bit of water that He sent down from the sky.

So, first what I'll do is I will explain the parable, the example itself. Then I will tell you what Allah is telling us behind the scenes of this example. So He says, 'a little bit of water that We sent down from the sky'. *Fa-khtalaṭa bihī nabāt al-arḍ*—then this water, because of it, the twigs and the plants of the earth start intertwining with each other. So trees grow and more trees grow and the roots are getting intertwined with each other and their branches are intertwined. You don't know where one tree ends and the next tree begins. Plants grow and shoots are wound into one another. This image is given because if you have a piece of land that is not very fertile, if you have a farm that's not very good, then you have a twig here and a twig there; a branch here and a branch there. They are far apart from each other but when all the plants are intertwined it actually means that there is a lot of greenery, it's a really good garden. Where every plant is just meshing into every other plant, it's blending into every other plant.

So Allah is talking about something that is extremely fertile; land that's extremely fertile. It's interesting, because Allah began with a little bit of water and then talked about a lot of fertility. What Allah is teaching us is that He gives you a little bit of *rizq*, a little bit of benefit, and as a result of that you start benefitting tremendously. You don't even know how those doors open for you. Allah will send your way one friend, one contact. Those of you that are in business, you started your business with very little money; you started your business with a hundred bucks, and you made one contact, you made one sale, and then it grew and it grew and it grew. One thing is intertwined with the other, one contact with another, one lead to another, one sale to another and that hundred dollars is now a couple of million dollars. But it's that same little bit of water from the beginning that creates all of that growth and allows for all of that growth to happen. One plant rises, another plant gives a hundred seeds, and those seeds go back into the ground, and then they are going to come up again. So this continual growth in our *rizq* from very, very little is from Allah.

Some people, they take pride, they say, 'you know when I started my business all I had was my laptop, all I had was a hundred dollars, all I had were the clothes on my back and then I made some smart investments', and they tell you their success story. Allah is telling us what happens even before that success story. He didn't just say that there is a little bit of water and a lot of plants grew, He said a little bit of water that *We* sent down from the sky, then a lot of plants grew. In other words, even your initial investment: where did you get it from? Where do you think you got it from? You started taking pride? With so little and look at how I made it grow. Allah says that so little wasn't even yours, I gave it to you. I started your business; you didn't start your business. I started your career; you didn't start your career. I helped you grow. *Fa-khtalaṭa bihī nabāt al-arḍ*. So now this garden is impressive. And, by the way, the example that was just given in the surah was about a garden. And so He says *fa-aṣbaḥa hashīman*—beautiful words—He says then over time it became *hashīm*. *Hashīm* in Arabic is something that is cut up, something that is dismembered. You know when you pull a little piece of a branch off, or snap a twig that becomes *hashīm*—it's broken up. There's a tree or a plant and you pull off a leaf then this leaf becomes *hashīm*, it's cut off from the rest, and this leaf is now useless. It doesn't have life any more. You can't give it life again, it's dead.

So Allah says these plants that grew, then out of nowhere they became useless, they became *hashīm tadhrūhu al-riyāḥ*—and they became so useless that the winds can throw them around where ever they want. And not just one wind Allah says *riyāḥ*—multiple winds. One wind takes them this way and another wind takes them another way. It's a very interesting parable. Recently I was in Seattle, I was just walking around in one of the market places and they had an antique store. I walked into an antique store and you see all this old stuff from the sixties, the forties, the twenties. You see a 1920s radio, you look at that radio and you start thinking: man, there was a time when this was the most expensive thing. There's going to be a time when somebody's going to walk into that antique store and there is going to be an iPad sitting there and people are going to be like: 'Oh, that is old. Wow, people used to use that thing?' It's going to be like that, right? It's going to be an antique.

And what happens to those things you buy? You use them until they become old then, they go into your closet, or they go into your attic. Then from your attic, you're moving and you just give it as a donation to somebody. And it goes around and around and ends up in the antique store, right? And why does it go around so much? Nobody wants to hold onto it, they just want to get rid of it because it's worthless. Allah compares the things you own that are so valuable to you right now, but in just a little bit of time, they are going to be in some attic. They are just going to be passed around by people until they are going to end up in a trash dump. They are going to be moved around from here to here to here; that same plant that was so beautiful, so lush, you walk into that place and it's a garden and then you come back and you realize that entire garden is gone, it's dried up twigs and the winds have taken those twigs from here to there to there. You don't even know where they end up—*tadhrūhu al-riyāḥ*. *Wa-kān Allāh ʿalā kulli shay'in muqtadirā*—and Allah has always been in complete control over all things. The word *fa* here—as opposed to *thumma*—needs to be highlighted. In the Arabic language when you say: *fa-aṣbaḥa hashīman*—that means over time the plants deteriorated; it took a long time before the plants died and then they became useless. *Fa* actually means *mufāja'atan*—it just happened, out of nowhere.

You know what Allah is telling us? It could be that you and I have wealth, we could be doing well and you might look at your wealth and say, '*Al-ḥamd li-Llāh*, I think I'm secure. I'm doing pretty good. I don't have to worry about money anymore'. But you know what? That sense of security is exactly the problem of the gardener that was talked about before. He thought: *lan tabīda hādhihī abadā*—'This ain't going nowhere'. Literally, that's what he said. He looked at his garden and said, 'Come on! This is too good an investment. Everything is exactly where it is supposed to be, my projections for sales are getting higher and higher. I'm hiring more and more employees. Things are looking pretty good. It's not going anywhere'. And what does Allah do? Overnight, his entire garden's gone. Overnight!

In this example it's greenery. In fact, it's not just greenery; it is so green that the plants are intertwined with each other. You're like, 'How's this going to go away? This is really fertile'. Then, all of a sudden, it becomes useless. It's just something people step on, people don't even care for, and winds carry it around. And when winds are throwing something around obviously it's accessible to everyone. Twigs and leaves and little pebbles on the ground, everybody has access to them, right? It's not like, you have to pay for them. Nobody picks them up and puts them in their pocket, because they are worthless. You don't see dollar bills flying around in the air, because there's a value to them. People will pick them up. Allah is teaching us that the things we own will one day be useless, they will just be useless. *Wa-kān Allāh ʿalā kulli shay'in muqtadirā.*

ٱلْمَالُ وَٱلْبَنُونَ زِينَةُ ٱلْحَيَوٰةِ ٱلدُّنْيَا ۖ وَٱلْبَٰقِيَٰتُ ٱلصَّٰلِحَٰتُ
خَيْرٌ عِندَ رَبِّكَ ثَوَابًا وَخَيْرٌ أَمَلًا ﴿٤٦﴾

(الكهف ١٨ : ٤٦)

Wealth and children are an adornment of the life of the world. But the deeds of lasting righteousness are the best in the sight of your Lord in reward, and far better a source of hope.

(Al-Kahf 18: 46)

Now after this example of gardens and plants growing, Allah (*subḥānahū wa-taʿālā*) then teaches us: what am I really talking about? If you didn't get the point yet, let me not speak in examples anymore, let me be explicit and direct with you. *Al-māl wa-l-banūn zīnat al-ḥayāt al-dunyā*—money and children they are the beautification, they are the beauty of worldly life. They are what make this low life beautiful. This life, right here, Allah boils it down to two things that are beautiful. Allah first says money, then He says children. And you know what? You talk to a young man who isn't married or who just got married, just starting his career, just finished school, first pay cheque that came through, right? What's he always thinking about? He's thinking about money and how to spend it. And if it's not money like cash, it's something that is a result of the money. It's the car, it's the furniture, it's the gadget in your pocket, right? It's the stuff that came from money, at the end of it, all of it is *māl*. *Māl* doesn't just mean dollar bills, *māl* means everything that the dollar bills got you. The apartment, the vacation, the clothes, everything; this is all *māl*. That's what you are obsessed with. You don't even have to ask them. A young man picks me up from the airport, he picks me up in his BMW and he says, 'Yeah, just got it a couple of years ago'. I didn't ask. But that's okay because you're obsessed, I understand. You have to let me know, but that's cool because Allah tells us that you are obsessed with that beautification of worldly life through wealth.

Then you meet older people and they may be driving a much more expensive car; they don't talk about their car they say, 'My son, *al-ḥamd li-Llah*, he's going to medschool. *In shā' Allāh* he's going to be a doctor soon. My other son, he's memorizing Qur'an'. All old people do this to me, they talk about their kids, because that's their joy. These kids may not even be good kids to them, they don't even call them; but they're still proud of them, they still bring them up. 'My son is doing this, *mā shā' Allāh*, he's done this, he's a lawyer', 'He's doing pretty well, he's doing his PhD', etc. They are always taking pride in their children. Even if their children aren't in touch with them anymore because the only beautiful thing left of you now is your children. Allah boiled the entire life of a human being down—*al-māl wa-l-banūn zīnat al-ḥayāt al-dunyā*. What's interesting about the example before? Allah mentioned his *māl*; the guy had a garden and He also mentioned—*ana akthar minka mālan wa-waladan*—I have children too. So, Allah says:

Al-māl wa-l-banūn zīnat al-ḥayāt al-dunyā, wa-l-bāqiyāṭ al-ṣāliḥāt khayrun ʿinda Rabbika thawāban—subḥān Allāh. He says: and the things that last, the few things that will last, that's how you have to translate *al-bāqiyāṭ*, this is a plural that means little (*jamʿ qillah*), so in a simple English translation that would mean, and the few things that are going to last—Allah is already telling us children won't last and money won't last—let me tell you the very few things that will last, what are they? *Al-ṣāliḥāt*—the few good things that you did; the few good deeds that you pulled off, that is what's going to last.

Khayrun ʿinda Rabbika thawāban—they are much better, in the company of your Master, as far as compensation is concerned. There is a treasure in this phrase: *khayrun ʿinda Rabbika thawāban*. Number one: it's better. Better for whom? Better for you. But Allah even adds—*ʿinda Rabbika*—Allah says because of those good deeds, not only are these good deeds better as far as Allah is concerned, these good deeds will allow you to be *literally* close to Allah. Allah will put you with those that are close to Him in *jannah*, and *then* He will pay you. Before He mentioned *thawāb*, He mentioned *ʿinda Rabbika*—He mentioned His closeness first and the compensation second, as though the closeness to Allah is a bigger reward than what we get in *jannah*. What we get in *jannah*, the house, the luxury, the joys, the pleasures, the beauties of *jannah*; all of that is *thawāb* but before *thawāb*, let me tell you about *ʿinda Rabbika*—in the closeness to your Master but from your Master's perspective. Then you get that *thawāb*.

Wa-khayrun amalan—and it is better, what a beautiful conclusion. And these few good things that you will do are also better—*amalan*—in terms of putting your hopes in them. *Amal* in the Arabic language means long-term aspiration. You have a little bit of money in the bank, you constantly go every couple of days, maybe every day, you log in and look at the balance and you say, 'Okay, I'm going to put this money over here. I'm going to use this one to do that, I'm going to use this one to do this. In a couple of years I'll buy this property. Maybe I'll extend the house a little bit more, maybe I'll put a pool in the back yard, maybe I'll do this, maybe I'll do that', you have all these plans. I'm going to pay the kids tuition from this money. I'll keep the investments over here—we're constantly thinking about the long term. What do you hope to do long term with this, this and this.

Allah says: yes, you can have long term hopes about your education, where you're going to get a job, where you're going to move, where you are going to live. You can have long term hopes about what kind of car you're going to get, what kind of house you're going to live in, what kind of business you're going to start. You can have long term aspirations, but let me tell you the few good things that you have done, you should have long term aspirations with those deeds because those deeds didn't die. That *ṣalāh* you made on time; it didn't die. That *ṣalāh* is alive and it will come back to benefit you on Judgement Day. That brother you helped out, who was in need, who didn't even ask and you helped out, on your own. That is an investment you made with Allah and it will not die. You don't have to login and check on it again. Allah is growing it, Allah is growing that investment. That one good bit of advice you gave, you pointed somebody in the right direction like the Prophet (*ṣallā Allāh ʿalayhi wa-sallam*) says—*al-dāll ʿalā al-khayr ka-fāʿilihī*—someone who points to something good is like the one who did it himself. Someone benefitted from that; those are investments you and I made for our *ākhirah*—*khayrun ʿinda Rabbika thawāban wa-khayrun amalan*.

Now as I conclude, I will leave you with these last words. The entire imagery so far has been about things that get planted into the earth; about things that come out, and then they become worthless, and then the winds just move them around. Then Allah says now you should think about yourselves; you have been planted on this earth. The things you own and how they're going to be moved around; you're not going to keep them forever. What does Allah (*ʿazza wa-jall*) say after this beautiful example, this powerful example? He says:

وَيَوْمَ نُسَيِّرُ ٱلْجِبَالَ وَتَرَى ٱلْأَرْضَ بَارِزَةً وَحَشَرْنَٰهُمْ فَلَمْ نُغَادِرْ مِنْهُمْ أَحَدًا ﴿٤٧﴾

(الكهف ١٨ : ٤٧)

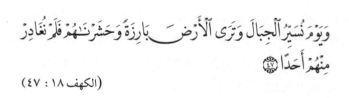

> Bear in mind the Day when We shall set the mountains in motion and you will find the earth void and bare. On that Day We shall muster all men together, leaving none of them behind.
>
> (Al-Kahf 18: 47)

Wa-yawma nusayyir al-jibāl—and a day will come, forget about plants moving around with the winds, the day on which we will make the mountains sail. When mountains are going to be uprooted, forget about plants. *Wa-yawma nusayyir al-jibāl wa-tarā al-arḍ bārizah*—and you will see the earth bare, it will expose what it really has inside—*wa-tarā al-arḍ bārizah. Wa-ḥasharnāhum*—and we will herd them like animals—*wa-lam nughādir minhum aḥadā*—and we will not leave anybody behind. Nobody will be excused from that herding and that gathering together.

وَعُرِضُوا۟ عَلَىٰ رَبِّكَ صَفًّا لَّقَدْ جِئْتُمُونَا كَمَا خَلَقْنَـٰكُمْ أَوَّلَ مَرَّةٍۭ ۚ بَلْ زَعَمْتُمْ أَلَّن نَّجْعَلَ لَكُم مَّوْعِدًا ﴿٤٨﴾

(الكهف ١٨ : ٤٨)

> They shall be brought before your Lord, all lined up, and shall be told: "Now, indeed, you have come before Us in the manner We created you in the first instance, although you thought that We shall not appoint a tryst (with Us)".
>
> (Al-Kahf 18: 48)

Wa-ʿuriḍū ʿalā Rabbika—and this is literally the example of the farmer; when the crop is ready, he plucks the plants. We've been planted into this earth like seeds go into this earth; all of us are going to go into this earth, right? We are going to go into this ground and then the harvest season will come. The harvest season is the Day of Judgement, and Allah will pluck every one of us out of our graves like plants are plucked out by the farmer when it's harvest season and stacked in rows. *Wa-ʿuriḍū ʿalā Rabbika*—they will be made to present themselves; they will be presented before your Master—*ṣaffan*—in rows upon rows upon rows. There is going to be this huge assembly of humanity and Allah will say then: *laqad ji'tumūnā kamā khalaqnākum awwala marrah*—you have come back to Us the way We created you the first time around. *Bal zaʿamtum an lan najʿala lakum mawʿidan*—and you had assumed that you don't have any meeting with Us, you thought you're not going to come back, you were hanging out in the world like there are no consequences. Do you think that right now—*bal zaʿamtum an lan najʿala lakum mawʿidan*?

وَوُضِعَ ٱلْكِتَـٰبُ فَتَرَى ٱلْمُجْرِمِينَ مُشْفِقِينَ مِمَّا فِيهِ وَيَقُولُونَ
يَـٰوَيْلَتَنَا مَالِ هَـٰذَا ٱلْكِتَـٰبِ لَا يُغَادِرُ صَغِيرَةً وَلَا كَبِيرَةً
إِلَّآ أَحْصَىٰهَا ۚ وَوَجَدُوا۟ مَا عَمِلُوا۟ حَاضِرًا ۗ وَلَا يَظْلِمُ رَبُّكَ أَحَدًا ﴿٤٩﴾

(الكهف ١٨ : ٤٩)

> And then the Record of their deeds shall be placed before them and you will see the guilty full of fear for what it contains, and will say: "Woe to us! What a Record this is! It leaves nothing, big or small, but encompasses it". They will find their deeds confronting them. Your Lord wrongs no one.
>
> (Al-Kahf 18: 49)

Wa-wuḍiʿa al-kitāb—and then the book will be placed, it will be put down—*wa-tarā al-mujrimīn mushfiqīn mimmā fīhi*—then you are going to see criminals that are just terrified about what this book has in it. Their book is dropped down and it's about to be opened, it's about to be read, people that did wrong in this life are just terrified that this book is about to be opened. They're going to say, 'Oh my God, this couldn't get any worse. What is wrong with this book? What kind of book is this?' *Mā li-hādhā al-kitāb lā yughādir ṣāghīratan wa-lā kabīratan illā aḥṣāhā*—it doesn't leave anything small out; it doesn't leave anything big out. No small detail got overlooked, no one thing I said, no one comment I made, no one post I posted; none of it got overlooked. None of it got erased. It is recorded completely.

Aḥṣāhā is used in Arabic when you count by putting pebbles in a bottle. This was an ancient way of counting. If you put pebbles in a bottle, the pebbles ain't going nowhere. They are in there now. The criminal starts looking at his book, 'Man, this book covered everything.

Stuff I remember and stuff I don't even remember. It's reminding me of what I did—small mistakes and big mistakes, small deeds and big deeds'. *Wa-wajadū mā ʿamilū ḥāḍiran*—and they will find whatever they have already done, standing right in front of them. Allah gave us two parables: on the one hand He said the few good things you've done are going to be a good investment for you. On the other hand He says the small bad deeds and the big bad deeds, if you don't care about your good deeds, then watch out because they are all going to be recorded and your deeds are going to be like this personified thing standing in front of you, face to face, like a mirror. *Wa-lā yaẓlim Rabbuka aḥadan*—and your Master is not going to do wrong to anybody. Nobody's going to wonder why am I being thrown into Hell? Nobody will wonder; they will know exactly what they did. Every little detail, so before they go, they will know.

The final comment about this *āyah* as I close, *in shā' Allāh taʿālā* is that, in this world sometimes you have secret courts and secret trials and people are sentenced to prison but when they are sentenced to prison you don't know what the evidence was; why were they considered a criminal? All the evidence is secret, we don't even know. When it's secret somebody could say, 'Well, they are probably innocent that's why they are keeping it a secret', right? Because secret trials usually mean there is going to be some kind of corruption. If you have nothing to hide, make it open. Same way in a classroom; you fail a student, he gets an F and you don't even show him his exam. Student says where is my exam? 'No, no you got an F', 'But can I see what my mistakes were?', 'No you can't see, you just got an F. You failed! Get out'. 'Let me see what I did at least!' If you don't show him what he did and he failed then he might think, 'He just hates me, he failed me. That's why he failed me because he doesn't even want to show me my deeds'.

Allah says: no, no, no. I will show you every last detail of what you did—*ṣāghīrah wa-kabīrah*—small and big, and He started with small ones, the small things. Because you and I think the only things that are going to be on our record is the big stuff. Little things on a day to day basis: who cares? He started with the small things. He started with that, and He said I'll show you first, then the Judgement, so you have no complaints about how We reached this Judgement, *subḥān Allāh*.

May Allah (*ʿazza wa-jall*) make us of those who really understand the value of this life and how this life is supposed to be an investment towards our *ākhirah*. May Allah (*ʿazza wa-jall*) make us of the people who are not shy to advise one another and give each other counsel about the temporary nature of this life. May Allah (*ʿazza wa-jall*) not make us a people of *dunyā* but rather make us a people of *ākhirah* who put this *dunyā* to work to build their *ākhirah*.

CHAPTER 13

Naṣīḥah in Brief: The Afterlife

In these few remaining paragraphs I want to share with you a reminder about the early revelations of the Qur'an. One of the themes that is highlighted more than perhaps any other in our *dīn* is the concept of the afterlife: the Day of Judgement, Paradise, Hellfire, the Reckoning, the world coming to an end and us being raised again for another life after this one. It's a recurring theme, it keeps coming up over, and over again and is discussed in a lot of detail. The question arises why? What are the benefits of having that as the main central discourse in Islam and especially in the early revelations when the foundations of the faith were being set.

Essentially the idea is captured in, for example, one place in the Qur'an:

كَلَّا بَلْ تُحِبُّونَ ٱلْعَاجِلَةَ ۝ وَتَذَرُونَ ٱلْآخِرَةَ ۝
(القيامة ٧٥: ٢٠-٢١)

Nay; the truth is that you love ardently (the good of this world) that can be obtained hastily, and are oblivious of the Hereafter.

(Al-Qiyāmah 75: 20-21)

Kallā bal tuḥibbūn al-ʿājilah wa-tadharūn al-ākhirah (*al-Qiyāmah* 75: 20-21)—No indeed! You love to rush, human nature is that it loves to rush. We like to consume things and get things to come our way quickly, especially good things; or we want bad things to be removed from ourselves quickly, immediately. So this mentality was challenged, and as a result of which you like to put the eventual thing off and even the afterlife off. So if somebody tells you,' You should worry about your salvation', which is obviously a concern after you die, you respond: 'Well, I got bigger things right now to worry about; I got a job, I got finances, I got family issues, I got personal things. Whatever I have to do right now is a bigger priority for me as opposed to whatever is coming later'.

So what the Qur'an does is it gives us a bigger picture, in other words nothing I do is any longer trivial, it's no longer meaningless. Allah says:

أَفَحَسِبْتُمْ أَنَّمَا خَلَقْنَٰكُمْ عَبَثًا وَأَنَّكُمْ إِلَيْنَا لَا تُرْجَعُونَ ﴿١١٥﴾

(المؤمنون ٢٣ : ١١٥)

Did you imagine that We created you without any purpose, and that you will not be brought back to Us?

(Al-Mu'minūn 23: 115)

A-fa-ḥasibtum annamā khalaqnākum ʿabathan wa-annakum ilaynā lā turjaʿūn (*al-Mu'minūn* 23: 115). It's very interesting, Allah says 'Have you assumed that We created you without purpose, and that you won't be returned to Us?' In other words, returning to God in itself is a very powerful indication that everything you do has purpose. My actions don't die with time; whatever I do, its consequences are recorded and they are going to have repercussions in this world and especially repercussions in the next. Some of the benefits of this are, of course: Firstly, it makes me conscious of my actions. I start thinking not just of the consequences they're going to have here but later on also. It removes from me the idea that nobody saw what I did. That's gone. God saw what I did and it's on record and I'm going to have to answer for it. Secondly, there will be accountability for everything that I do. Thirdly, I realize that as a result I have to keep turning back to God for forgiveness, because there are a countless number of mistakes I make all the time. So it makes me a person that seeks God's forgiveness all the time, seeks Allah's forgiveness. As a result I become closer and closer to Allah, closer to God. So the concept of the afterlife actually drives me to become closer to Allah, because the focus in Islam is always Allah. It goes back to Allah every time. Even if the conversation is about Paradise or Hellfire, the point of it is to take us back to Allah, Himself.

Finally and most importantly, we don't think of anything as trivial. In other words, we don't think of our time in this world as trivial; this little bit of time that we have on this earth, compared to the actual life span that Allah has given me, determines everything. In other words when He, Almighty, created me—this is even before the creation of generations of people. Our souls (*arwāḥ*) were created, and one of them is picked by the angel and dropped into the belly of a mother so that she can deliver this child; but all of us are created before even the earth and we were asked a question about our faith even before we came to this earth. Then after we die from here we are going to go into another state of life, and it's going to go on for generations. For some people, that life in the grave that they are going through, they've been going through it for thousands of years. They've been in there. That's another phase of life. We don't see it as death; we see it as another stop in the journey of life.

So when you compare all these stops in the journey of life you will realize that *this* life, meaning from my birth to my worldly death, is the shortest stop in this journey—the shortest span. When you realize that, then you also realize this tiniest space, this tiniest lifetime that I have, this will determine all of my future. My eternal life is based on these very few moments, so my time is no longer trivial. I have to make the best of it; I have to make the most of it. There is no such thing as free time for me now. What the afterlife does is give me respect for my time. A sense of urgency to accomplish more and more good and to get away from more and more evil; it destroys laziness inside me. So, if I find, and if you find yourself being lazy then you have to ask whether or not your beliefs in the afterlife are concrete enough. Maybe you need more reminders about the afterlife because they necessarily give you a sense of urgency. And for those of you who think, 'Well, Judgement Day, Paradise, Hellfire, it's so far away', what does Allah Himself say:

إِنَّهُمْ يَرَوْنَهُۥ بَعِيدًا ۝٦ وَنَرَىٰهُ قَرِيبًا ۝٧

(المعارج ٧٠: ٦-٧)

(6) Verily they think that the chastisement is far off,
(7) while We think that it is near at hand.

(Al-Maʿārij 70: 6-7)

Innahum yarawnahū baʿīdan wa-narāhu qarīban (*al-Maʿārij* 70: 6-7)—no doubt they see it far away; We see it near. I hope this reminder, and the reminders that preceded it, were of some benefit to you. I personally benefit from reminding myself that all of us have to rejuvenate ourselves to better use our time, especially through a reminder of the *ākhirah*. May Allah give all of us success in the afterlife.

Wa-ākhir daʿwānā an-al-ḥamd li-Llāh
Rabb al-ʿālamīn.

Glossary

ʿAbd-Allāh: Male servant of God.

Abū Sufyān*: One of the leaders of the Quraysh who eventually accepted Islam at the Conquest of Makkah.*

Aḥkām (sing. ḥukm)*: Legal rulings, typically in relation to the Shariah.*

Ākhirah: Means the Hereafter, as opposed to this world.

ʿAlayhi al-salām: Meaning "peace be upon him," recited as a prayer after the mention of prophet's name who came before Muhammad.

Al-ʿAlīm: One of God's Names meaning "the All-Knowing".

Al-ḥamdu lil-Lāh: Meaning "all praise is due to God".

ʿalim (pl. ʿulamaʾ): An Islamic scholar.

Al-Masjid al-Nabawī: The Prophet's Mosque in Madinah.

Al-salāmu ʿalaykum: Islamic greeting meaning "peace be upon you".

Amānah: "Trust", in the sense of something that is entrusted to one's care.

Amat-Allāh: Female servant of God.

Āmīn: Amen.

Amīr al-Muʾminīn: Commander of the Believers.

Astaghfir Allāh: Meaning "I seek God's forgiveness".

Āyah (pl. Āyāt): Has multiple meanings including sign or indication, the phenomenon of the universe, miracles performed by the Prophet and the individual or a verse from the Qur'an.

Āyat al-Kursī: the Verse of the Throne (al-Baqarah 2: 255).

Ayyūb: The Qur'anic prophet known in English as Job.

ʿAzza wa-jalla: "be He Glorified and Majestic," recited or written after the mention of God's name.

Banī Isrāʿīl: The Children of Israel.

Barakah (pl. Barakāt): Blessing.

Bāṭil: Null and void.

Battle of Aḥzāb: One of the last major battles fought by the Muslims against the Quraysh after the hijrah to Madinah.

Battle of Badr: The first major battle fought by the Muslims against the Quraysh after the hijrah to Madinah.

Battle of Uḥud: The second major battle fought by the Muslims against the Quraysh after the hijrah to Madinah.

Bi-idhn Allāh taʿālā: Means "with the permission of God, the Exalted".

Chacha: Paternal uncle.

Dīn (pl. Adyan): Means religion, Islam as a complete way of life and also divine recompense in the Hereafter.

Duʿā': Prayer or supplication.

Duʿāt (sing. Dāʿī): Preachers or callers to Islam.

Dunyā: Meaning this world, as opposed to the Hereafter.

Durūs (sing. Dars): Lessons.

Faḍl: Virtue or benefit.

Fajr: The name of the dawn prayer. The original Arabic literally means "dawn".

Farḍ: Legally binding or obligatory. It applies to such Islamic obligations as the five daily prayers.

Fatihah: The name for "the Opening" Surah of the Qur'an.

***Faqīr* (*pl. fuqarā'*)**: The poor, a person who depends for his subsistence on others.

Fatwa: An Islamic legal ruling.

Fiqh: The science of Islamic law, i.e. the collection of rules that make up Islamic law.

Fir'awn: Pharaoh.

Fitnah: Means "trial", "test", "civil strife" and "insurrection".

***Fuqahā'* (*sing. Faqīh*)**: Jurists or legal scholars with expertise in Fiqh.

Ghībah: backbiting.

Hadith (pl. aḥādīth): Referring to reports from the Prophet, typically exemplifying his teachings.

Hajj: Pilgrimage is one of the five pillars of Islam, which is compulsory once in a lifetime for those Muslims who can afford it.

Halal: Permitted in Islamic law.

Ḥamzah: An uncle and Companion of the Prophet (S). After his death, the Prophet granted him the title Master of the Martyrs (sayyid al-shuhadā').

Ḥaqq: "Right" and "truth".

Ḥaram: The sacred precinct of the grand mosque of Makkah, surrounding the Ka'bah, the Prophet's Mosque in Madinah and the Aqsa Mosque in Jerusalem. This word should not be confused with the Arabic word *ḥarām*, which has been adopted into English as haram, meaning "prohibited".

Haram: Forbidden or prohibited in Islamic law.

***Ḥawāriyyūn* (*sing. Ḥawārī*)**: The epithet given to the disciples of the Prophet 'Īsā.

***Ḥikmah* (*pl. Ḥikam*)**: Wisdom, or wise saying.

Hind: The wife of Abū Sufyān. Both were initially completely opposed to the Prophet and fought him bitterly, but would eventually accept Islam after the Quraysh were defeated in the virtually bloodless Conquest of Makkah.

Ibrahīm: The Prophet Abraham.

'Ilm: Knowledge.

Imam: Prayer leader; also refers to a religious leader in a more general sense.

Īmān: Means "faith" or "belief".

In Shā' Allāh: God willing

'Īsā: The Qur'anic prophet known in English as Jesus.

'Ishā': The Islamic prayer held after nightfall.

Ismā'īl: The Qur'anic prophet known in English as Ishmael.

Istighfār: Seeking forgiveness.

Jahannam: Hellfire.

Jannah: Paradise.

Jazā': Recompense.

Jazāk Allāh khayran: Expressing gratitude, literally meaning "may God reward you".

Jumu'ah: Friday congregational prayers obligatory for Muslim males to attend.

Kalām: Speech.

***Kabīrah* (*pl. Kabā'ir*)**: Grave sin or enormity.

Khāla: Maternal aunt.

Khālid Ibn al-Walīd: An extremely effective military commander from the Quraysh who led them in the Battle of Uḥud, but later converted to Islam, and subsequently led the Muslim army to many victories.

Khaṭīb: A person who gives a khuṭbah or sermon.

Khayr: Good(ness).

Khuṭbah: Typically the sermon given by the imam as part of Friday and eid prayers.
Kūfī: Cap worn by some Muslims.
Kufr: Disbelief.
Kuffār (*sing. Kāfir*): Disbeliever.
La'nah: Curse.
Ma'ādh Allāh: "God forbid!".
Maghfirah: Forgiveness.
Mahr: A gift promised by a bridegroom to a bride as a part of an Islamic marriage contract, which thereby becomes her property.
Mansūkh: "Abrogated", referring to the phenomenon where later revelation occasionally rendered a previously revealed ruled to be no longer applicable.
Ma shā' Allāh: Islamic phrase meaning "what God willed".
Masjid (pl. Masājid): Muslim place of worship, the mosque.
Miskīn **(pl.** *Masākīn*): Meaning poor person or beggar.
Mufti: An individual qualified to issue Islamic legal judgments (fatwas).
Mu'min: Believer.
Mūsā: Prophet Moses.
Musāfir: Traveler.
Mushrik (*pl. Mushrikūn*): One who associates partner's with God, such as idol-worshipers.
Nikah: An Islamic marriage.
Nūḥ: Prophet Noah.
Qirā'ah: Reading or recitation of the Qur'an.
Quraysh: The name of the tribe into which the Prophet Muhammad (S) was born in Makkah.
Rabb: Refer to God, usually translated as Lord.

Raḍiya Allāh ʿanhu: Phrase uttered when the name of a Companion of the Prophet is mentioned or written, literally meaning "may God be pleased with him".

Raḥmah: Mercy.

Ramadan: The ninth month of the (lunar) Islamic calendar during which Muslims fast.

Rasūl: Messenger of God.

Rizq: Provision.

Rūḥ: Spirit, soul.

Rukūʿ: The bowing position in Muslim prayers.

Ṣabr: Meaning patience or perseverance.

Ṣadaqah: Charity.

***Ṣaḥābah* (*sing. Ṣaḥābī*)**: Companion of the Prophet.

Ṣalāh: Muslim prayer conducted five times a day. One of the five pillars of Islam.

Ṣallā Allāh ʿalayhi wa-sallam: The prayer recited after the mention of the Prophet's name, meaning "may God's peace and blessings be upon him".

Sayyi'āt: Bad deeds or sins.

***Shahīd* (*pl. Shuhadā'*)**: A Muslim martyr.

Sharʿī: Pertaining to the Shariah

Shariah: The Islamic legal tradition that is seen as encapsulated in the scholarly discipline of fiqh.

***Shayṭān* (*pl. Shayāṭīn*)**: Devil.

Sīrah: The biography of the Prophet Muhammad.

Shirk: Associating partner's with God.

Shukr: Gratitude or thankfulness.

Subḥān Allāh: Glory be to God.

Sunnah: literally means "way", "path", or "norm". In a more technical sense, it refers to the practice of the Prophet. It can also refer to supererogatory practices, such as extra prayers prayed in addition to the obligatory ones.

Surah: A chapter from the Qur'an.

Taqwā: Piety, God-consciousness, or fear of God.

Tawakkul: Referring to the concept of reliance on God.

Tawḥīd: The doctrine of the oneness of God.

Tijārah: Trade or business.

Umar: The name of the second Caliph of Islam, Umar ibn al-Khaṭṭāb.

Ummah: The global Muslim population understood as a single community of believers.

Umrah: The non-mandatory lesser pilgrimage performed in the Haram of Makkah.

Ustādh: Teacher.

Wa-ʿalaykum al-salām: Response to the Islamic greeting, al-salāmu ʿalaykum, the translation of which is "and upon you be peace".

Walā' and barā': "Loyalty and disavowal", namely the notion that one's Islamic commitments necessitate loyalty to certain values, and a rejection of others.

Walī (sing. awliyā'): Referring to the male guardian of a woman, often in the context of marriage, who is typically her father.

Wal-Lāhi: An expression for swearing by God.

Wilāyah: "Guardianship", usually in the context of marriage.

Yawm al-Qiyāmah: The Day of Resurrection.

Yūnus: The Qur'anic Prophet known as Jonah.

Zakat: An obligatory payment of 2.5% made by those who can afford it on an annual basis under Islamic law. This is one of the five pillars of Islam.

Zakariyyā: The Qur'anic prophet known in English as Zechariah.